ACKNOWLEDGEMENTS

It is difficult to remember all of the many people who, over the course of the last 10 years, have helped me gather information about our country's wonderful provincial and national parks. This book has been researched with the help of an eclectic group that includes fellow campers, friends, and parks staff and officials, who, although they have remained nameless, have given me their time, experience, and knowledge during site visits and through numerous telephone calls and e-mails. I am indebted to all of these people.

The excellent staff at Heritage House Publishing Company continues to offer support and constructive criticism. Heritage House first suggested the idea for this book more than five years ago; I hope it lives up to expectations.

This text would not, of course, have been possible without my two wonderful sons, Jack and Sam, who completely and unknowingly have shown me a totally new side of camping and a refreshing way to experience life outdoors.

Finally, my best friend and camping and life partner, Andrew Dewberry, continues to support my enthusiastic ambitions and goals and remains my *raison d'être*.

Jayne Seagrave

Jack and Sam are happy campers.

CAMPING
with Kids

The Best Family Campgrounds in British Columbia and Alberta

Jayne Seagrave

Heritage
House

Copyright © 2004 Jayne Seagrave

National Library of Canada Cataloguing in Publication

Seagrave, Jayne, 1961-
    Camping with kids: the best family campgrounds in British Columbia and
Alberta / Jayne Seagrave.

ISBN 1-894384-55-5

    1. Camp sites, facilites, etc.—British Columbia—Guidebooks. 2. Camp
sites, facilities, etc.—Alberta—Guidebooks. 3. Family recreation—British
Columbia—Guidebooks. 4. Family recreation—Alberta—Guidebooks. 5.
British Columbia—Guidebooks. 6. Alberta—Guidebooks. I. Title.

GV191.46.B75S424 2004   796.54'085'09711   C2004-900024-1

First edition 2004

Heritage House acknowledges the financial support for our publishing program
from the Government of Canada through the Book Publishing Industry
Development Program (BPIDP), Canada Council for the Arts, and the British
Columbia Arts Council.

Cover and book design by Darlene Nickull
Edited by Terri Elderton and Karla Decker

Front cover: Family campsite.
Back cover: Top, Rathtrevor Beach Provincial Park; middle, Buttle Lake
(Strathcona Provincial Park); bottom, Ellison Provincial Park.
All photos provided by the author unless otherwise noted.

HERITAGE HOUSE PUBLISHING COMPANY LTD.
Unit #108 – 17665 66A Ave., Surrey, BC V3S 2A7

Printed in Canada

BRITISH
COLUMBIA
ARTS COUNCIL
We acknowledge the support of the Province of British Columbia
through the British Columbia Arts Council

The Canada Council | Le Conseil des Arts
for the Arts | du Canada

CONTENTS

HOW TO BE
A HAPPY CAMPER

Since January 8, 1999, my world has not been divided into black and white, rich and poor, old and young, fat and thin, but rather has been split between those who do and those who do not have kids. For 10 years I camped in B.C. with only my spouse (and occasionally the province's mosquito population) for company. Since having children, there are times when I wonder if the mosquitoes would be preferable to my two young sons. As a mother I know you are not supposed to say that children radically change your life—but they do. And they've certainly altered my camping life.

In 1998 my publisher, upon learning of my pregnancy, asked whether I'd write a book about camping with kids. In 1999, after spending five nights in a tent with my eight-month-old, I told him the book would consist of one word: DON'T. Five years and another child later, I realize that a lot of fun can be had while camping with kids, if you carefully choose the campground and invest some time in planning.

This book includes what I believe are B.C.'s best provincial and national park campgrounds for camping with kids, as well as a small selection of those in Alberta. Almost all of these campgrounds accept reservations and are, for the most part, close to a centre of population with medical services and a fast-food restaurant, yet still foster that get-away-from-it-all experience. They also usually offer water-based activities, which can be the biggest draw for kids.

During much of the year, our time as parents is committed to school, daycare, and piano, swimming, soccer, or hockey lessons. Evenings and weekends are usually consumed with just the basics of preparing meals, cleaning, running errands, and supervising homework. Camping is a wonderful, economical way to enjoy our children in a different and stimulating environment. There are tremendous bonuses in travelling with your children to an unknown destination, in living outdoors and sleeping in the same tent under the stars, and in sharing their enthusiasm when experiencing the country from a totally new perspective.

The boys decide what to take camping.

Children who spend time in different locations also expand their awareness of the world, and they bring an energy and exuberance to new experiences. They have no social barriers and make friends easily and quickly. As your kids get older, they will find new pursuits, new friends, and new experiences.

I believe camping is a gorgeous way to escape the city, meet others, learn about the outdoors, and have an adventure. Children will often remember their camping adventures for the rest of their lives. I have found that no two camping trips are ever the same, even if we return to the same campground year after year. Each camping adventure is totally unique, and that is why I adore it.

At the time I wrote this book, the provincial parks system in B.C. was undergoing numerous changes. Many of the services that regular campers have come to know, such as free firewood, free parking, interpretive programs, and campground hosts, have now been cut or are under review, while other services—campground concession stores, for example—are being added. Thus, writing this book was somewhat challenging. Fortunately, the unique geography each park offers can't be changed.

Family Camping

What you can and cannot do when camping with kids depends on the age of your offspring, as each age brings unique experiences, joys, and challenges. For example, having preschoolers means long hikes are out, but you don't have to change diapers anymore. Babies are portable and can be nicely packed away, but can crawl into everything if left on their own.

The family enjoys a picnic in Bear Creek Provincial Park.

Camping while Pregnant

Strangely enough, few books on pregnancy touch on the topic of camping while pregnant. Each woman experiences pregnancy differently; some breeze through it while others have a hell of a time. I had many good nights sleeping in a tent when I was eight months pregnant and would say that if you're feeling up to it, do it.

The only problem I had camping while I was pregnant was the number of bathroom trips I had to make in the middle of the night, which meant squatting while balancing an extra 30 pounds in front. Toppling over and trying to right yourself, semi-naked in the dark at 2:00 a.m., does make you realize why heavily pregnant women may wish to think twice about camping, or at least opt for the campsite nearest to the toilet. Remember also to pack plenty of pillows to support the bump if you're sleeping in a tent.

Camping with Babies or Toddlers

If your baby is not yet a crawler, camping is easy. Okay, you do have to take more stuff, but you can leave the baby happily goo-gooing in the car seat on the picnic table while you erect the tent. A playpen can be used as a crib, and a mosquito net can be easily laid over the top, should bugs be a problem.

Camping with toddlers, however, is another matter. This age can be the most challenging because of all the equipment they require, their need for diapers, and

Happy camper Sam relaxes in his playpen.

their propensity to put everything in their mouths. The great outdoors, replete with animals, rocks, stones, water, dirt, vegetation, and insects, can't be childproofed as easily as can your home. I believe the secret to camping with toddlers is being relaxed about it. So they don't have a wash before going to bed, or they sleep in the clothes they've been in all day, or they delight in treading on the ants and poking the banana slugs with pine cones; let them do it. The biggest problem I found while tent camping with toddlers was in their early-morning waking. The dawn arrives and their excitement over seeing you sleeping next to them stimulates their delight and curiosity; so you get up at 5:30 a.m. and experience the campground at a time few others will. Afternoon naps may also be a challenge if you try to get them to sleep in the unfamiliar tent. A better option is a gentle push in the stroller around the campground's roads, especially if these are gravel—an almost surefire way to send them to sleep.

Most of the difficulties of this tent-based experience are, of course, avoided by camping in a recreational vehicle (RV), camper, tent trailer, or towing trailer. If there is ever a time when you get rid of the tent and choose an RV, it is at this age (see "How to Camp").

On the plus side, kids of this age are still quite portable, so you can hike with them in a backpack—something that is not an option with the preschooler.

Camping with Preschoolers

While you can't send these young ones off to explore the campground on their own, children at this age are a real delight to take camping. The under-fives can actively get involved with camping and what it means to set up home outdoors away from the urban centre. They can help select flat ground to put up the tent, get sticks for toasting marshmallows, explore adjacent undergrowth without eating it, take a ride on the tricycle, and run around and make noise. Expect them to stay up late, get dirty, make friends with the kids from the next campsite, play the best imaginary games, and have a ball.

Camping with this age group also means you can vacation in May, June, or September and avoid the crowds and the added expense. Make the most of it and remember to teach them your campsite number upon arrival, as well as basic safety information (see "Camping Safely"). Also remember to pack fishing nets, water shoes, and plastic toys.

Jack looks out the back door of his home away from home.

Camping with Preteens

By setting boundaries and following a few simple rules, children this age will learn to love the camping experience. Provincial and national parks provide wonderful safe environments for children to explore by themselves. Parents do not have to worry about unsafe roads and fast drivers, video arcades, or TV. Children can gain some independence by learning and exploring safely on their own. Parks are fantastic for cycling, rollerblading, swimming, and exploring with new-found friends, or with friends brought from home. Remember their board games, crayons, sidewalk chalk, balls, bikes, rollerblades, and books, and they will be sure to entertain themselves. The big disadvantage for this age group is the restriction of having to camp during school holidays and weekends, when parks are most crowded. A little planning ahead helps a lot, though; these are the times when you really appreciate the reservation system (see "Reservations").

Camping Safely

When you arrive at a campground, remember to teach your children to memorize the campsite number. BC Parks and the Royal Canadian Mounted Police offer guidelines on what children should know while in the woods through the "Hug a Tree" program, which started in San Diego and has been adopted across North America. Here are some highlights from this program.

Hug a Tree and Survive

1. Tell your parents where you are going, with whom, and when you plan to return.
2. Stay on well-marked trails and always hike with a buddy.
3. Wear brightly coloured, warm clothing and bring a hat.
4. Carry a garbage bag and whistle (a garbage bag can be used to keep you warm if you get lost, and a whistle attracts attention and can be heard from further away than a voice).
5. Carry a non-perishable snack and drink.
6. If you get lost, hug a tree—it can help you feel better and offers shelter. It will also keep you in one place so you have a better chance of being found.
7. Help people find you. Don't hide if you see someone looking for you.
8. Stay calm. You will feel safest and stay calm if you stay in one place. If you hear a noise that frightens you, yell out your name—animals tend to be more scared of you than you are of them.
9. Make yourself big. Try to pick a tree near a clearing so you can be easily seen.

(See the website at
www.rcmp.ca/ccaps/hug_e.htm
for more information.)

How to Camp

Tent, RV, or Motel?

In spite of having a two-and-a-half-year-old and a nine-month-old, being constantly stressed and exhausted, and reaching my 40th year, I believed I'd found my true nirvana in July 2001: a 24-foot GO WEST rented motorhome. Okay, some women dream of diamonds, others of convertible BMWs, and more wish for spouses who do not spend 40 minutes in the bathroom at one time, but for me life could not have improved the moment I sat in those brown, heavily cushioned, velour seats of my first rented RV. Camping would never be the same again. I had reached middle age, and if accepting it meant being comfortable in my watertight, warm, and air-conditioned RV, then so be it.

I had camped in a tent the previous year with my 18-month-old son, while I was eight months pregnant. Camping was a challenge. A year later we took our motorized home to Alice Lake Provincial Park, to Lillooet, and then back down Highway 1 to Vancouver. The kids sat opposite each other in raised seats at the back of the camper, totally contented. Music could be played directly to them, and we were free to enjoy the scenery without listening to Raffi for the millionth time. There was a fridge, microwave, two large double beds with sheets and duvets, a toilet and shower, even space for the playpen. And the disadvantage … a night in an RV during the high season was costing the same as a night in a four-star Whistler hotel.

Jack's ready to build a fire.   *Sam heads into the RV.*

I found nirvana in a 24-foot rented motorhome.

Recreational vehicles are not cheap to rent (or purchase and maintain), especially during the peak seasons of July and August. They do make the camping experience with kids a lot easier and just as enjoyable, and there are some good deals to be had if you go during the shoulder seasons of May, June, or September, or if there are enough adults to share the expense. (Remember, there is nothing to stop the adults from sleeping inside and letting older children camp under canvas outside.) When my children were toddlers I really appreciated the darkness the RV offered (no waking at 5:00 a.m. with the dawn birds as they had done in a tent), the confinement of the loud crying fits (fellow campers also appreciated this), the fridge for keeping milk cool or the microwave for warming food, and the instant "afternoon nap" on the road, which we all were able to enjoy. If you can afford it, camping in an RV when your children are under three is highly recommended.

Camping obviously requires more than just a tent, and all the extra equipment can be costly, depending on what you decide you need. (I cover the basics in "What to Take Camping.") If you have never camped before and do not want to invest in all the gear only to find you are definitely not a camper, consider one of two options. Option one is to borrow the tent and gear from a friend. I would like to say that nothing much can go wrong with borrowing equipment, except that we loaned our tent and self-inflating mattresses to some novice campers a few years ago, and while they were asleep, their small dog, who was also in the tent, started to bark. To discover why the dog was excited they unzipped the tent only to find a skunk outside, which then proceeded to do what skunks do best—spray the tent. Our tent spent the next week soaking in tomato juice in an effort to get rid of the damage. The other option is to rent equipment. Mountain Equipment Co-Op (604-872-7858 in B.C., 403-269-2420 in Alberta) rents tents, mattresses, sleeping bags, and even kid carriers. It also offers a weekend special from 3:00 p.m. Thursday until 1:00 p.m. Monday when you pay for only two days, so you can see whether you and your family are indeed camping material. I understand Canadian Tire is also considering renting out camping equipment in the future.

Finally, I have to add that there is nothing wrong with deciding you (or your spouse or offspring) are not always the camping types and opting to stay in a lodge or motel.

For example, I have camped at Alice Lake, but have also enjoyed this park as a day visitor and stayed at the Mountain Retreat Hotel and Suites in Squamish, which has an excellent kids' waterslide and pool. Likewise, I have enjoyed camping at Manning Provincial Park for two nights and then spent the third night in the park's lodge. During our last family visit to Lakelse Provincial Park, we visited the provincial park for only a few hours and spent most of our time at the hot springs resort 3 kilometres down the road.

Many of the stresses of camping (or of just being in constant close confines with your nearest and dearest) can be relieved by spending a night in a motel complete with air conditioning, TV, temperature-controlled showers, kitchens, laundry, and, of course, a soft bed. There is nothing wrong with combining camping and motel stays, and organizing your holiday to incorporate both.

Regardless of your lodgings, there are some wonderful provincial and national parks to experience with your children, even if you do not camp in them.

Trailer camping: a tent serves as an extra bedroom.

What to Take Camping

Each camper has his or her own idea of the camping essentials. Even if you think you've covered every eventuality, this thought is probably naive. I don't think I've been on a camping trip when I haven't forgotten something, but that's the fun of it all.

As our boys grew older, we invested in a two-dome tent with an interlocking connection. This tent effectively has two rooms, both with a separate entrance. Each dome can be erected separately, but also connected to the other to form two adjoining spaces—ideal when camping with young children whom you may want to easily see. When shopping for a tent, check out what Canadian Tire has to offer. This store offers a great range of products for family camping.

We all sleep on self-inflating mattresses that roll up tightly and are easy to pack, but which also provide a good night's sleep. Our children sleep in full-sized sleeping bags (which they find great fun, calling them "slug-sacks"), but we still prefer to pack up our duvet and sheets for a good night's rest. If you put young children in full-sized sleeping bags, you may want to include extra blankets (fleece is ideal) as they do tend to move out of the bags.

After 13 years of camping, I've found the best way to store and transport my camping gear is in large plastic containers: one for cooking utensils and crockery, one for our mattresses, one for food (non-perishable), and one for other stuff (flashlights, hibachi, foil, axe, insect repellent, tarps, matches, etc.) Of course, we also take a large cooler and a camp stove. The first time you camp, you'll take too much and forget all the important things, but with more experience, you'll get better at knowing what to take and what you don't need. Remember, in most cases you can buy whatever you need as you travel.

Eating outside is a wonderful experience and, of course, just being outside makes you hungry. We purchase enough food for about three days, because after this time, even with the best cooler, fresh food tends to get a little ripe. Our staples are the clichéd hot dogs and marshmallows, supplemented by sweet corn, fresh vegetables and dips, and fruit. We also have pita pockets, tortilla wraps, pasta, crackers, cheese, bacon, cereal, granola bars, and fruit bars, Other necessities include milk, juices, water, and the odd beer to keep the chefs hydrated. I always include non-perishables such as tins of pasta, tuna, and baked beans, and, of course, copious quantities of tomato ketchup.

We often eat breakfast out because the children tend to wake up early. Many of the provincial park campgrounds have breakfast restaurants, or coffee bars serving baked goodies, within a 10-kilometre drive.

My "What To Take" List

The Kid List

Fishing nets (our family uses these to catch "toe-biters," my father's name for small fry)

Fishing rods

Sand toys (stored in a string bag so the sand drains away between visits to the beach)

Bug collection kit (often available at dollar stores)

Flashlight (my kids really like the ones that they can wear on their heads, good for trips to the washroom when it's dark, while older kids love reading by flashlight in the tent)

Books	Compass
Magnifying glass	Sidewalk chalk
Baby change pad	Crayons, pencils, paper
Water shoes	Life jackets

My "Also Remember" List

First-aid kit, including calamine lotion, DEET, sunscreen

Garbage bags/plastic bags (lots of spare ones if your kids are in diapers)

Aluminum foil	Axe
Backpack	Barbecue, hibachi, gas stove, and gas
Bowl for washing dishes	Bungee cords
Camera and film	Candles and lantern
Flashlights	Food
Maps	Matches and newspaper
Paper towels and wet wipes	Plastic containers for food
Pots, dishes, cutlery	Rope
Sleeping bags and mattresses	Sunglasses and hats
Swiss army knife	Tarps
Tent	Tissues
Toiletries	Towels
Water container	

What to Expect at a Provincial or National Campground

National and provincial park campgrounds are well signposted on major highways. The first warning campers receive is a sign posted 2 kilometres before the campground turnoff, and another sign 400 metres from the campground. The second sign gives directions to the access road. If a campground is full or closed, the park operator will post notices on these roadside signs stating this fact.

Located near provincial park entrances, these information boards provide a map of the campground and warnings about area hazards.

If you have a reservation at a campground (see "Reservations"), your reserved site will be listed at the park entrance. For those without a reservation, the biggest thrill upon arrival at a campground is deciding which spot to settle in. Occasionally, in the larger campgrounds and in Alberta, parks staff pre-selects the sites. Depending on the season, time of day, and location of the park, your choice of spaces could be limited. Some parks have areas specifically designated for tents, while most provincial and national parks have spots suitable for either RVs or tents. A number of parks offer "double spots," ideal for two families camping together, and pull-through spots for the larger RVs. There is usually a map of the campground at the entrance detailing where these spots are to be found.

Once you have established which sites are restricted, you will need to "cruise" the campground so you can pick a spot. Campsites by a beach, lake, river, or creek are most desirable, so head for these first. Avoid areas of stagnant water (mosquito breeding grounds) or sites next to the "thunderboxes" (pit toilets), which may exude unpleasant odours, attract flies, and disturb you with the noise of banging doors. Sites near the flush toilets and showers may seem convenient, especially if you are pregnant or have young children, but the downside is that between 5:00 p.m. and 11:00 p.m. and again from 7:00 a.m. to 11:00 a.m., most people at the campground will be visiting these facilities and walking past your site in order to get there.

As you drive around the campground, make note of your preferences and then claim your most desirable spot by parking a vehicle there. Alternatively, leave some item, such as a water jug or a plastic tablecloth, on the picnic table to state to the world that this spot is taken.

When you are established in your new home, you are ready to explore the campground. Remember to tell your children the campsite number and, if possible, a reference point (e.g. near the big tree, just by the amphitheatre). Your first stop should be a return to the information board at the campground entrance, as this will have a full map of the campground, details of any hazards in the area, information about other campgrounds in the region, and, if you're lucky, leaflets and maps.

You will want to familiarize yourself and your kids with the facilities available at the campground. All provincial and national park campgrounds included in this book have the basics: flush toilets, water, wood (for sale), pit toilets, picnic tables, and firepits. Larger campgrounds might have showers, baby-change facilities, sani-stations, wheelchair access, visitor centres, and group camping. Washroom facilities are generally well maintained and clean. Gravel camping spots are tidied and raked after each visitor departs, garbage is regularly collected, and there are bins for recycling.

A park attendant collects fees (cash only) during the early evening hours and sells firewood. As you might expect, camping fees vary depending on the facilities provided; campgrounds with showers tend to be the most expensive while less developed campgrounds have lower fees. At the time of writing, fees ranged from $9.00 to $22.00 a day for provincial parks and up to $24.00 for national parks (GST included). Firewood costs between $5.00 and $7.00. You can stay for as many nights as you want, up to a maximum of 14 nights in both provincial and national parks. The attendant will post a receipt at your spot that displays the date you intend to leave. Although some campgrounds are open throughout the year, fees for individual camping spots are only collected from April to October.

The park attendants who collect fees are good sources of information on weather conditions, local activities, the best fishing locations, and so on. They also tend to be interesting characters, attributable perhaps to the long periods of time they have been working outdoors, operating what one described to me as "a huge open-air hotel."

Washrooms/showers

The biggest reason people resist camping is undoubtedly because of the rougher washroom facilities. Having spent the first 30 years of my life in Europe, where finding toilet tissue in the washroom of a downtown pub after 8:00 p.m. is a luxury, I am amazed by the notion some people have that BC Parks washroom facilities are unpleasant. Granted, a pit toilet in a popular provincial park in the heat of July is not a good place to read your favourite novel, but in spite of the slightly unpleasant odours and the flies, it will have been cleaned within the last 12 hours, so there will be plenty of toilet tissue.

There are basically three types of toilets in provincial and national parks. The first are the pit toilets—"thunderboxes"—boxes painted white inside, centrally located in various sections of the campground. The second type of toilet looks like a thunderbox but houses an odour-free flushing toilet. The third type is the conventional washroom with sinks; some of them contain showers. BC Parks staff cleans and services all three types of facilities twice daily.

The typical thunderbox, or "pit toilet" is clean, but is not a place to linger reading your favourite novel.

The larger washrooms have mirrors that almost without exception give a distorted, unclear image, so do not expect to be able to apply makeup in front of one. The water temperatures in some campground showers may be a bit erratic, but they are generally adequate, and, unlike those in many private campgrounds, do not cut off after you have had the allotted two minutes and still have shampoo in your hair. Some campgrounds have family shower rooms and, increasingly, baby-change facilities—but don't expect these.

Water is available either from a conventional water faucet or from a pump. Collecting water from a pump is a bit of an art (expect to get wet feet, but to delight your children), and, in certain parks, will give your arm muscles a good workout. You may want to include a funnel with your camping gear, as it can help considerably when you are collecting pump water.

Garbage/recycling

You can tell if a campground is in an area inhabited by bears by the look of the garbage bins. If they are swinging barrels or elongated metal cylinders with tight lids and a catch, you can be sure there are bears around. Provincial and national parks do recycle, although the extent of recycling varies between parks. Remember that you should never leave garbage at your campsite, as it attracts racoons, chipmunks, skunks, crows, and even bears. I remember vividly the night (B.C.—Before Children) when we retired to our tent a little the worse for wear due to the litre of wine we had consumed with dinner, only to be awakened at 1:30 a.m. by the sound of wild creatures ripping through our belongings. Raccoons had discovered our garbage, which we had neglected to take to the bins, and in the early hours were having their own noisy picnic. From where we were lying in the tent, these animals sounded more like huge moose than little raccoons. Now, no matter how mellow we feel, we always remember to dispose of the garbage.

A note on bears: B.C. is bear country, with a quarter of the black-bear and half of the grizzly-bear population in Canada. Campers should never approach or feed bears (see "Potential Hazards: Bears"). Food-conditioned bears—those that scavenge food from garbage cans and picnic tables—begin to associate food with people, lose their natural fear of humans, and become a threat to campers and to themselves.

During a visit to Wells Gray Provincial Park in the summer of 1998, I was fascinated to read details of bear sightings near the popular Clearwater Campground, where we were camped. I noted that the most recent had been three days before our arrival, at campsite number 28. As we were at site number 12, I felt quite safe. Being five months pregnant, I had a night punctuated by numerous trips outside the tent. The following morning I awoke to find a huge pile of very fresh bear scat at the entrance to our site. A black bear had passed within feet of our tent during the night while we were asleep, or while I was squatting in the bushes. This was a good reminder to us to exercise caution and be aware of this very real hazard.

Recreational activities

Activities offered at the park will vary, of course, depending on the size and location of it. Many parks have boat launches, safe swimming areas, cordoned off for children (but have no lifeguards), hiking trails, adventure playgrounds, horseshoe pits, volleyball nets, large grassy areas for ball games, and amphitheatres. Occasionally interpretive programs

Amphitheatres provide ideal meeting places for every age. Most of the campgrounds in this book have access for the disabled, as well as camping spots specifically designed for those in wheelchairs. Many trails are wheelchair (and stroller) accessible.

are offered, or programs specifically designed for children, but these kinds of services are being cut back or privatized, so whether or not a park has them depends upon the park's administration.

Parks staff

Parks workers are usually delightful characters with unique personalities and idiosyncrasies. As the people responsible for these "huge open-air hotels," their job is to keep the washrooms clean and tidy, garbage cleared, and campsites clean; to collect fees; and, of course, to ensure we all remain happy campers. What a lovely task. They wear blue shirts and shorts or trousers (brown in national parks), and are frequently an unbeatable source of information about the surrounding areas. They can also be useful in helping the novice camper light a campfire or suggesting the best place to pitch a tent.

Reservations

One of the biggest camping success stories is the reservation system, introduced in 1996 by BC Parks. It allows campers to reserve spots at the more popular provincial and national parks in B.C. With the exception of Waterton National Park in Alberta, all of the campgrounds detailed in this book accept reservations.

The advantage of reservations is that they assure accommodation for the night. For those with children, or with commitments that prevent an early getaway for a camping weekend, the reservation system does away with uncertainty and ensures that the joy of camping is not denied. However, unlike the system operating in Washington State where clients select their own spot, the B.C. service gives campers no say over the spot designated to them. You could find yourself located next to a well-used thunderbox, at the busy entrance to the campground, or at a particularly small site. But you will have a site.

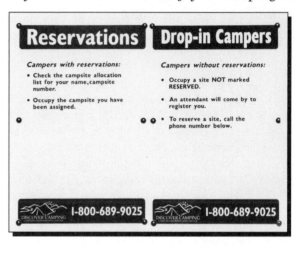

To make a reservation in B.C., phone Discover Camping Campground Reservation Service at 1-800-689-9025 between 7:00 a.m. and 7:00 p.m. (Pacific Time) Monday to Friday and between 9:00 a.m. and 5:00 p.m. on Saturday and Sunday. This service is available from March 1 to September 15. At the time of writing, the fee to reserve was $6.00 per night to a maximum of $18.00 for 3 to 14 nights. This fee is subject to GST. Campers pay the reservation and campsite fees by MasterCard or Visa when making the reservation. You can reserve a site up to three months in advance, but a reservation must be made at least two days prior to your arrival at the campsite. You can cancel a reservation via voice mail or the Internet 24 hours a day.

Prospective campers can also check the availability of campsites at campgrounds that accept reservations on the Internet. If a space is available, you can book it by speaking to a Discover Camping representative or by booking on-line (www.discovercamping.ca). If you do not have a reservation, campsites are available on a first-come, first-served basis. When you arrive at a campground, a notice board at the gate will provide details on which spots are reserved. Only a percentage of campsites in each campground are reservable—although this can be as high as 75 percent—and I have often found that the best campsites are the reservable ones.

Camping Rules

There are a number of unwritten camping rules. For the most part they are common sense, and they exist to ensure all campers have a good time.

1. Quiet time is from 11:00 p.m. to 7:00 a.m. Provincial and national parks close their gates during this time to prevent arrivals from disturbing the peace.

2. In late summer or on island campgrounds, the threat of forest fires may result in a ban on campfires. Check park information boards to determine status. At all times, light fires only in metal firepits.

3. Store food in your vehicle or in airtight containers. With over 100,000 black bears in B.C., this is not a rule to ignore. If you do not have a vehicle and are in an area frequented by bears, hang food in bags suspended well out on a tree branch, at least four metres above the ground.

4. To protect plant life, camp only in the designated areas.

5. Reduce waste and recycle as much as possible. BC Parks provides dispensers for recycling.

6. Each year, campers in B.C. parks burn the equivalent of 2,000 logging trucks of wood. Wood should not be wasted; burn only as much as you need.

7. Checkout time is 11:00 a.m., and the maximum length of stay is 14 days per year in any one park. A camping party is regarded as a family from the same address or a maximum of four people 13 years or older, one of whom must be over the age of 16.

8. Cutting branches and picking flowers, berries, or mushrooms is prohibited in provincial and national parks.

9. Clean your campsite on departure, making sure all food remains and garbage have been cleared away.

10. Pets should be kept on a leash in all areas of the campground.

11. Do not use your firepit as a garbage disposal. Partially burnt food attracts wildlife, and blackened cans are an annoyance to the next camper.

12. Only one camping vehicle is allowed per campsite. This vehicle must fit comfortably without damaging the location or causing a nuisance to other campers. The only exceptions are when an additional vehicle is being towed, or when group members arrive from a common home address in separate vehicles (the commuter vehicle must be registered at the same address as the registered party).

13. Do not take powerboats near swimmers. Try to avoid disturbing the tranquillity of those enjoying the beach by revving engines excessively.

14. Alcohol is not permitted in the public areas of B.C. parks but *is* allowed at your campsite.

Potential Hazards

At the entrance to each campground, you will find a list detailing any hazards in the campground. Here are some common hazards, including ones particularly dangerous for children:

Swimmer's itch

Parasites living in freshwater snails and waterfowl can cause swimmer's itch, or *cercarial dermatitis,* a temporary skin irritation caused by the parasite's larvae entering the skin. The larvae thrive close to shore in the warm waters of lakes and ponds, often where Canada geese and other fowl are found. Because children go in and out of the water often and have tender skin, they are particularly vulnerable. Swimmer's itch can be avoided by applying skin oil (baby oil is a good choice) before swimming, towelling off briskly, and showering after swimming. Swimmer's itch develops as small red spots that can develop into blisters. Although unpleasant, the symptoms can be treated with calamine lotion and the condition usually clears up by itself within a week.

Poison ivy

This low, glossy plant with three green leaves and white berries can produce severe skin rashes. It is prevalent on Vancouver Island and in the Okanagan. Calamine lotion is an effective treatment.

Sunburn

By its very nature, camping means being outdoors from sunrise to sunset, so make sure your children wear a hat and are protected by sunscreen. Special UV-protected swimwear is available that covers the whole body—an expensive but effective option. If you're near water, reapply sunscreen often. Remember that water reflects the sun's rays and can compound the sun's effect on skin. Increase exposure to the sun gradually, and remember to keep well hydrated.

Water

B.C. and Alberta parks do not have lifeguards, so keep a watchful eye on young children. Some parks have designated shallow swimming areas; others do not. It is the parents' responsibility to ensure their children's safety around water. When boating, you are required by law to carry properly fitting life jackets, or, for infants weighing between 20 and 30 pounds, Personal Flotation Devices (PFDs), which are worn more like a vest, have more flexibility, and are designed for situations where the swimmer can be rescued quickly. Many parents purchase a PFD specifically for their child's play near water; good ones should have a label showing the Canadian Coast Guard approval and weight guidelines. When non-swimmers play in or near water, it's good to establish rules; for example, they can go into the water only up to their chest, or stay within calling distance of you.

Bears

B.C. has almost one-quarter of all the black bears in Canada and about half of the grizzlies. Although people-to-bear encounters are extremely rare, campers should always remember they are in bear country. Generally, bears go out of their way to avoid people, but all bears are dangerous, and those with young cubs are especially so.

Anyone planning to enjoy the outdoors should learn how to recognize a black or grizzly bear and how to respond accordingly. Black bears can be black, brown, cinnamon, or blond with short, curved claws, and a small shoulder lump. Grizzly bears can also be black, brown, or blond, are bigger than black bears, have long, curved claws, and a prominent shoulder hump. If walking in bear country, watch out for warning signs

Don't feed the bears. (Heritage Collection photo)

such as overturned rocks, bear scat, clawed trees, and chewed roots. Talk loudly, wear bear bells, or sing to make your presence known. If you encounter a bear at close range, avoid eye contact, move away slowly, and stay calm. If the bear approaches standing up, it is trying to identify you. Talk quietly so it knows you are human. If it is lowering its head, snapping its jaws and snorting, it is displaying aggression. This is serious. Do not run but continue to back away. If a grizzly shows aggression, consider climbing a tree. Generally the key is to do nothing to threaten or arouse the animal. If a grizzly attacks, play dead by adopting a tight, curled-up position with your head on your knees and your hands behind your head. Do not move until the bear leaves the area. If a black bear attacks, try to retreat; if this is not possible, fight back with rocks, sticks, and branches to deter the animal.

Never approach or feed bears. Food-conditioned bears begin to associate food with people and lose their natural fear of humans, becoming a threat to campers and themselves. With caution and sensible behaviour you can safely camp and enjoy bear country.

Bugs

I have found these to be far more common in Alberta and the northern parts of B.C. than in the Okanagan, Lower Mainland, and on Vancouver Island, which is something to bear in mind when planning a trip. The most effective way to keep the mosquitoes and blackflies at bay is DEET, but it can be irritating to children and should not be used on babies under six months old. The Canadian Paediatric Society suggests children between six months and 12 years of age use repellent containing no more than 10 percent DEET. This solution provides three hours of protection. Soybean oil has also been found to be an effective, non-chemical repellent and was recently sanctioned by Health Canada. Mosquito nets for strollers are available from good camping stores and Canadian Tire.

Fire

Children should be taught to keep well away from the firepit and that it can remain hot even when the fire has gone out. Toddlers especially need to be watched closely if you are using the firepit.

Camping Tips

One of the joys of camping is learning the little tricks that make it easier. Here are a few tips:

1. If you do not have a reservation, try to arrive at a campground before 5:00 p.m., as the busiest hours for arrival are between 5:00 p.m. and 8:00 p.m.

2. If the campground does not have a shower, leave a full plastic water container in the sun all day long and wash in warm water in the evening.

3. Take a water container and a funnel to collect water from the pump.

4. Use bungee cords hooked between trees as clotheslines.

5. Cook vegetables (e.g. mushrooms, tomatoes, zucchini, peppers, and onions) by wrapping them in aluminum foil, sealing them in with spices.

6. It's a good idea to keep a key-ring-sized flashlight in your pocket for emergencies and for nightly excursions to the washroom.

7. Axes, matches, dry paper, plastic bags, rope, flashlights, candles, and aluminum foil are all camping basics.

8. Spread a tarp under the tent for extra protection against the damp.

9. Keep one set of clothes specifically for wearing by the campfire so you have only one outfit smelling of woodsmoke.

10. Dry wet wood by propping logs against the firepit.

11. Take folding chairs, as they are far more comfy to sit in (and if you're breastfeeding, these chairs are a must).

Now you are ready for a camping adventure ... GO FOR IT!

How to Use This Book

This book has been divided into five chapters. The first three describe campgrounds in the most populated areas of B.C.: the Lower Mainland, Vancouver Island and the Gulf Islands, and the Shuswap/Okanagan. The next chapter details four campgrounds in the more remote areas of the province, including northern B.C. and the Rockies, and the final chapter provides a little taste of the best campgrounds in Alberta.

Each campground entry contains a number of subheadings. After the introduction, an historical account of the area is provided. The "Location" subsection describes how to find the campground, and the "Facilities" subsection describes the services offered at the park. Under the subheading of "Recreational activities" I include hiking, swimming, cycling, fishing, wildlife viewing, and family activities. "Rainy-day activities" include things to do near the campground. The "Summary" subsection provides personal and anecdotal information. We have camped as a family in all the campgrounds listed, with the exclusion of Lakelse Provincial Park, where we stayed at the nearby Hot Springs Resort as it was May and too cold to camp. With the exception of Waterton National Park, all campgrounds can be reserved, so it is possible to plan a one-week or two-week camping vacation safe in the knowledge that you have a reserved space.

No privately owned campgrounds are included in this book. Although there are many privately run facilities perfect for family camping, my expertise is only with the government-owned parks.

As stated above, the provincial park system in B.C. is undergoing a number of changes, so some details may not remain accurate. Every attempt has been made to provide the most current and correct information.

A camper's home is his castle—at any age.

LOWER MAINLAND

With campgrounds in over 20 provincial parks across the Lower Mainland, it is a challenge to select the best. Although the following five are my own personal preferences because they are near centres of population or have showers, there are a number of others that are delightful places to camp (e.g. Birkenhead, north of Pemberton; Nairn Falls, north of Whistler on the Sea to Sky Highway; Porteau Cove, again on the Sea to Sky Highway, south of Squamish; and Saltery Bay on the Sunshine Coast).

Porpoise Bay on the Sunshine Coast is attractive if only because most visitors have to take a ferry to get there, so that cries of "Are we there yet?" are put to rest as children enjoy the 40-minute ferry ride. This boat excursion, the wonderful beach, warm temperatures, and proximity to Sechelt make Porpoise Bay a pleasant destination. Alice Lake, only 90 minutes from Vancouver, also has a wonderful beach, fantastic mountain scenery, and is very conveniently located near Squamish, should you require pizza or fries. Similarly, Golden Ears, the most popular campground in the province, provides all facilities and can also be reached by Vancouverites within a couple of hours. Further afield, Sasquatch Provincial Park, with its three distinct campgrounds and four lakes, provides wonderful family camping, and should the weather turn nasty, there is always the mineral-fed indoor pool in Harrison Hot Springs. Finally, three hours from Vancouver is Manning Provincial Park, a huge park with swimming, cycling, hiking, boating, horseback riding, and fishing opportunities. Every activity you could possibly want is offered here, again, amidst some wonderful scenery.

Porpoise Bay Provincial Park

My prevailing image of Porpoise Bay is of family-friendly facilities; excellent services; large, private, well-maintained wooded camping spaces; beautiful scenery, including a sandy beach; and a nearby town—perfect for a family vacation. Porpoise Bay is unique as it has a non-fire policy, meaning all firepits have been removed, thereby giving the camping spots a slightly unfurnished appearance. A notice on the park's information board explains the decision: "BC Parks has responded to requests by the community and some campers to improve the air quality by reducing the number of firepits in the park. At the same time, it is recognized campfires are a special part of the camping experience." Consequently, three communal firepits remain, so you can still roast a hot dog or toast a marshmallow and enjoy the experience of the campfire with other campers. I have camped here every year since I have had children, which is in itself a testimonial to just how good this place is and how accommodating to children of every age.

The wide sandy beach at Porpoise Bay is perfect for young children.

History

The original inhabitants of the area were the Shíshálh people, who hunted and fished in the region between the Strait of Georgia and Porpoise Bay. The name "Sechelt" is taken from this First Nation. In the 18th century, British and Spanish explorers roamed the coastline. In 1986 the local Sechelt Band became the first in Canada to be given authority to manage their land.

Location

Porpoise Bay Provincial Park is on the Sunshine Coast, which stretches along the northeastern side of the Strait of Georgia between Howe Sound to the south and Desolation Sound to the north. To reach this campground you take an excursion on BC Ferries from Horseshoe Bay, where an excellent kids' playground can be found beside the ferry terminal, should you arrive with time to kill. Catch the ferry from Horseshoe Bay to Langdale, a 45-minute sailing, and then follow Highway 101 to the centre of Sechelt (25 kilometres), where the paved, 5-kilometre Porpoise Bay Road leads to the campground. The 61-hectare park is located on the east side of the Sechelt Inlet.

Facilities

Campers here want for nothing, as Porpoise Bay has flush and pit toilets, showers, a sani-station, wheelchair access, and it also accepts reservations. There are 84 large, gravel camping spots, including a few double units in a second-growth forest of Douglas fir, western red cedar, western hemlock, and alder. As mentioned above, fires are prohibited in individual campsites but are permitted in the three communal pits between 5:00 p.m. and 10:30 p.m. The campground has an area specifically designed for camping cyclists, which can accommodate up to 40 people. All services are found 5 kilometres away in Sechelt, including a McDonald's (no play space, but there is a Megablocks play table) and a growing number of very good bakeries, coffee shops, and restaurants.

Recreational activities

Hiking

A number of trails ribbon throughout the park. The most popular is the Angus Creek Trail, which leads to a tree-lined stream that is a spawning waterway for chum and coho salmon in the fall. Interpretative boards describe this process. Another trail leads to the marsh area of the inlet. At low tide it is great to take the kids and just wander along the shoreline. Lifting stones reveals scampering crabs, and the rock pools offer small fish, shrimp, and jellyfish—great for the collection bucket (but remember to put them back).

Boating

The park functions as a base for kayakers who use it to explore the many coves and inlets of the surrounding area. Porpoise Bay is near the Sechelt Inlet Provincial Marine Recreational Area, which includes eight wilderness campsites located on the sheltered waters of the Sechelt Inlet—a paddler's delight. The area is also rich in marine life. Therefore, although Porpoise Bay is especially popular with families, those who like to paddle can also find tranquillity here amidst the West Coast scenery.

Fishing

When we last visited, we saw numerous fish jumping out of the water only a stone's throw from the swimming area. Fishing in the inlet and the various rivers and streams can yield coho salmon and cod. There are also fantastic opportunities for young kids to catch toe-biters with nets in the shallow waters of the protected swimming area.

Wildlife observation

Porpoise Bay is recommended as a wildlife viewing location by the Ministry of Water, Land and Air Protection's BC Wildlife Watch program. You are likely to see loons, grebes, cormorants, ducks, and bald eagles, especially if you are

The kids love to fish for "toe-biters."

34

walking around the campground first thing in the morning with young children. Information boards detail when each type of bird visits the park and your chances of seeing them.

Family activities

One of the biggest attractions here is the wide, sandy beach and the protected shallow swimming area, ideal for young children. A grassy field with picnic tables, toilets, playground, and change house is adjacent to the beach, and at suppertime this area is crowded with parents trying to exhaust their kids before bed. It's a lovely meeting place. There is a great field for all games in the centre of the campground, and a number of sites have direct access to it. When we last camped, our kids ran around this space and were taught *boules* (a French form of lawn bowling) by another group of older children while we cooked dinner. Float planes take off and land at the other side of the inlet, providing an interesting although somewhat noisy distraction.

Rainy-day activities

The nearby bustling community of Sechelt is a pleasant place to explore. One of the most impressive buildings in the town is the House of Hewhiwus (House of Chiefs), a massive cultural centre containing the offices of the Sechelt Indian Government District as well as a museum, theatre, and gift shop. The staff members at the brand new Sechelt Visitor Centre can give you advice on hiking, kayaking, fishing, diving, cycling, and golf in the area. You can take a lovely quiet drive up the Sunshine Coast north of Sechelt. Skookumchuck Narrows Provincial Park, at the north end of the Sechelt Peninsula, is well worth a visit, especially if you plan your arrival to coincide with the peak tidal flows. Alternatively, travel 25 kilometres south to the community of Gibsons, famous for the *Beachcombers* TV series and a quaint maritime museum.

Summary

Porpoise Bay is an excellent family campground, close to all amenities. Kids can have fun on a beautiful sandy shoreline, while adults can become frustrated at the expanse of shallow waters that make deep-water swimming a challenge. One real advantage here is the weather, which is dry, sunny, and moderately warm in summer (the average July temperature is 18 degrees Celsius), and mild in winter, with considerably less rain than elsewhere in the Lower Mainland—another reason to select this campground for a perfect family vacation, especially in the shoulder seasons of June and September. Many have recognized its advantages, so you should make reservations if you plan to camp in July or August.

Finally, I have to add that this is one of the quietest campgrounds I know. Even when it is full, everyone seems to be in bed by 10:00 p.m. I attribute this to the lack of campfires, which means that few noisy alcohol-induced conversations occur, as there are no glowing embers to congregate around. In sharp contrast to many other campgrounds in the Lower Mainland, Porpoise Bay is really quiet and for this reason, and a multitude of others, it should be on every camper's list of "must-visit" spots.

Alice Lake Provincial Park

Alice Lake is my favourite campground to escape to quickly. We can leave our home in Vancouver and be there in 90 minutes. In June and September, as long as it's not a hot weekend, we can easily find space, although chances of finding space in July and August are slim to non-existent. A Tim Hortons restaurant is only a 12-minute drive from the campground (this fact has been very well researched), should one decide to indulge in sandwiches and donuts under the stars. And yet, despite this urban access, Alice Lake still provides that get-away-from-it-all experience. This was the park in which all four of us first camped together under canvas, so I am romantically attached to it. We all went to bed at 7:30 p.m., giggled, and told stories in the tent until it got dark (8:30 p.m.—it was September), whereupon the kids went to sleep and we lay awake watching them in the half light, eventually being lulled to sleep by their breathing. Camping does create quite wonderful memories.

History

Alice Lake is close to the community of Brackendale, once larger than Squamish but now part of that municipality. Squamish, meaning "Mother of the Wind," has been settled since the late 19th century, when pioneers from Europe arrived to log giant cedar and fir trees that

Alice Lake is not far from Vancouver, but still provides that get-away-from-it-all experience.

were then tied together and floated across Howe Sound to the population centres farther south. Alice Lake was named after Alice Rose who, with her husband Charlie, was among the first settlers in the region. They built a homestead in the 1880s and earned a living by logging and farming. The provincial park was established in 1956.

Location

The park is easily accessible from Vancouver on Highway 99—the Sea to Sky Highway—13 kilometres north of Squamish. Nearby Brackendale is home to the largest population of bald eagles in North America. Visitors to Alice Lake have a good chance of seeing these splendid birds, but they are not the only attraction in this extremely popular park. There are also four lakes: Alice (the largest, covering 11.5 hectares), Stump, Fawn, and Edith.

Facilities

The 96 large, private, shady camping spots are suitable for all camping vehicles and are situated in a forest of western hemlock. There are also 12 walk-in sites. Paved roads ribbon throughout the campground, which is equipped with showers, flush and pit toilets, and a sani-station. Alice Lake offers disabled access and accepts reservations. There are a couple of small stores in Brackendale, and the growing community of Squamish has all services, including an excellent McDonald's with a play area where the staff come to your table to give the kids toys and top up your coffee. Additional supplies can be found along the highway between Squamish and the park (e.g. A&W, Tim Hortons, Canadian Tire).

Recreational activities

Hiking

For the ambitious, Alice Lake is a base from which to explore Garibaldi Provincial Park. Garibaldi covers almost 200,000 hectares and during the summer months you can hike to alpine meadows, glaciers, and mountains. Much of Garibaldi and the surrounding area is forested with fir, hemlock, red cedar, and balsam. In summer it displays a breathtaking blanket of alpine flowers, making hikes in the area well worth the effort. For the less adventurous, there are a series of walking trails at Alice Lake itself. One of the most popular is the Four Lakes Trail, an easy, 6-kilometre (two-hour) walk with minimal elevation gain that takes hikers around the four warm-water lakes dominating the area; it's varied and kids can easily complete it. Interpretative boards posted on the section around Stump Lake describe the area's natural history. Numerous physical reminders of past logging operations are clearly visible from the trail. Another trail leads up Debecks Hill. From here you can enjoy views of the area that was shaped by volcanic activity thousands of years ago.

Boating

All four lakes have paddling potential, with Alice Lake being the most popular site. Motorized crafts are prohibited on all lakes, which makes canoeing, kayaking, and fishing tranquil pursuits. Canoes can be rented in the park.

Cycling

A number of gravel roads that are attractive to mountain bikers run throughout the park. Some of the trails are closed to cyclists during the summer months, but are open at other times. The paved roads in the park are great for kids cycling and rollerblading.

Kids love to dig in the sand at Alice Lake.

The boys wade in the weed-free waters of Alice Lake.

Fishing

At the southern end of Alice Lake there is a pier, popular with fishers, from which you can cast your line for cutthroat, rainbow trout, and Dolly Varden. In May one year, we watched a father and his seven-year-old son catch nine trout from the children's swimming area in the space of 40 minutes. Quite a stunning sight, for, as most would agree, you never usually see fishermen catch anything. The three other lakes also offer fishing possibilities: Edith, Stump, and Fawn lakes are annually stocked with rainbow trout.

Family activities

Because Alice Lake is close to Vancouver, it attracts a great number of Lower Mainland families during the summer months—and for good reason. It has wonderful beaches for sunbathing or playing, clear weed-free waters for swimming, a large grassy area for ballgames next to the kids' beach, numerous picnic tables, and a change house. Swimming areas are cordoned off from the open lake, and there are wooden rafts to swim to. The beach, with its great sand for sandcastle building, is the main attraction, as is the view of the snow-capped mountains that encircle the lake. The waters of the lake can be cold … but when did that ever bother the under-five age group? There is an adventure playground nicely positioned in the shade, and as this campground does attract so many families it's the sort of place where your kids will make friends very easily.

Rainy-day activities

In recent years, the community of Squamish has grown, and now boasts several attractions, including a railway museum with a number of trains from a bygone age, some faithfully restored and others waiting to be returned to their former glory. One of the highlights of visiting this museum is the chance to speak to the volunteers and staff, who tell interesting stories about the trains' histories. There is also a really neat miniature railway to ride. It's easy to spend two to three hours here and is well worth a visit even if you're not camping. Squamish also has a golf course, a museum, and a number of commercial facilities that offer such things as helicopter tours of the nearby glaciers or whitewater rafting excursions.

The Tenderfoot Fish Hatchery is located just outside Brackendale and has exhibits of chinook, coho, and steelhead (free admission). South of Squamish is the B.C. Museum of Mining which is ideal for kids over the age of seven. Here you don hard hats and take a train ride underground for a really informative tour. North of the campground is Brandywine Falls Provincial Park, where a short walk leads to some spectacular falls. Finally, of course, if the weather is really bad, think of visiting Whistler, only an hour's drive further north, for a bit of window shopping and strolling. Here the Starbucks and Blenz coffee bars are located directly in front of the children's play area, so you can enjoy a cappuccino and watch the kids have fun too.

Summary

Alice Lake is a very popular location, even during the week, and is frequently full over the peak summer months, In June, it is already too late to reserve a camping spot for a weekend in July and August, so if you arrive during these times without a reservation, make sure you have a backup plan. One option is Nairn Falls Provincial Park, north of Whistler. It is not as popular as Alice Lake, but has camping facilities as well, and as long as you arrive before 5:00 p.m., you will have a good chance of finding a spot.

Golden Ears Provincial Park

By writing a guidebook listing "the best," an author is exposed to immediate criticism, since what one person sees as the best may not be perceived that way by another. However, Golden Ears records more camping parties each year than any other provincial park, making it the most popular provincial park with camping facilities in B.C. Its popularity is partly due to its location near a large centre of population. I can leave my central Vancouver home and be at my camping spot in Golden Ears within an hour (traffic permitting), and for those who live in other regions of the Lower Mainland the commute is even shorter. Consequently, this campground does receive what may be termed the "younger crowd," especially during weekends in June, and can become a little noisy.

History

There are two theories on how Golden Ears got its name. The first says it is named after the twin peaks of Mount Blanshard, which shine golden in the sunlight. The second says it was known as a nesting place for eagles—"golden aeries." Its history dates back thousands of years to the time when Interior Salish and Coast Salish people used the area around Alouette Lake as hunting and fishing grounds. During the early part of the 20th century this was the primary site for B.C.'s logging activity. The main logging company was Abernethy and Lougheed, which ran the largest logging operation in the area, at one time employing over a thousand men. There are stories of the company sending a cross-section of a red cedar measuring over three metres in diameter to England for the Empire Exhibition in the 1920s, and of felling trees up to four metres in diameter. A huge fire devastated the area in 1931 and put an end to the logging operations, although you can still see evidence of this industry today. (Check out the huge tree stump by campsite number C32 at Alouette Campground.) The area was purchased by the provincial government in the 1930s as an extension of Garibaldi Provincial Park, and in 1967 it was designated a park in its own right.

Location

Situated in the Coast Mountains between Pitt Lake to the west and Mount Judge Howay Recreational Area to the east, and dominated by the 1,706-metre Golden Ears Mountain, this 55,000-hectare park is a short drive (45 to 60 minutes or 48 kilometres) from Vancouver. It is located 11 kilometres north of Maple Ridge off Highway 7 on paved road access, and stretches over 55 kilometres from its northern boundary to Garibaldi Park at its southern end.

Facilities

Alouette and Gold Creek are the two well-maintained campgrounds in Golden Ears. The former has 205 spaces, the latter 138. A few years ago another campground, North Beach, was added with just 55 spaces (no showers). All have large, private spaces in wooded areas of Douglas fir, western red cedar, hemlock, and balsam. When we last stayed at Alouette my two kids adored "playing in the jungle" between the campsites and selecting sticks for toasting marshmallows. All facilities are wheelchair accessible, including showers, a baby change table in the shower buildings, flush toilets, and a sani-station. Reservations are accepted and advisable if you plan to visit in the peak summer months or on weekends. A full range of services is available in Maple Ridge, and there are also a few small stores, fast-food outlets, and a gas station on the access road adjacent to the park.

Are we there yet? Almost!

Recreational activities

Hiking

Trails range in length from easy hour-long strolls to full-day hikes. The magnificent Golden Ears Trail (24 kilometres return) is best undertaken during the long daylight hours of July and August. Only the fit should attempt this hike, and I would also recommend you take copious quantities of bug repellent if venturing on this excursion. For those seeking less arduous activity, there are a number of short, self-guided nature trails at the southern end of Alouette Lake and near the Alouette Campground. The longer Lower Falls Trail is particularly popular with families. This 2.7-kilometre easy walk is along Gold Creek to Lower Falls and passes along the beach, bestowing gorgeous views. The Alouette Lake Loop is a circular route around Mike Lake that takes about two to three hours to hike and covers approximately 6 kilometres. If you want a climb, the trail to Viking Creek Lookout is another alternative.

Horseback riding

The park is popular with horseback riders, as there is an extensive system of riding trails. You can arrange riding excursions through stables next to the East Canyon Trail. Mike Trail, East Canyon Trail, and Inline Trail are all open to horses.

Boating

Boat-launching ramps are available north of the day-use area, and powerboats are permitted on the lake. During the summer months you can rent a canoe from the day-use area and explore 18-kilometre-long Alouette Lake with its 30 kilometres of shoreline. This is reputed to be one of the best freshwater lakes in the Lower Mainland. Winds frequently develop around midday, so paddling is a more strenuous activity at this time. Canoeing allows you to escape from the crowds and explore some lovely quiet coves.

Cycling

Mountain bikes are permitted only on the park roads, Alouette Mountain Fire Access Road, and East Canyon Trail. There are negotiations underway to extend the number of mountain bike trails in the park. The campgrounds themselves have a maze of gravel roads that youngsters can explore by cycle; however, they can return from these rides quite dusty.

Fishing

Even though the lake is stocked each year with rainbow and steelhead trout, the fishing here is not great. Rainbow trout, coastal cutthroat, kokanee, char, and Dolly Varden can be found in Alouette Lake and River. Pitt Lake has a variety of fish and provides more diverse angling opportunities for cutthroat, rainbow, steelhead, Dolly Varden, and four salmon species, in addition to carp, catfish, and sturgeon.

Family activities

Alouette Lake's many sandy beaches are a delight for children. The most popular is Campers Beach, situated between the two campgrounds. Do not bother with a bucket and spade here, as it is a pebbly beach, but do pack the water shoes. My kids spent hours playing on the floating logs at this beach.

Another day, another marshmallow: it just doesn't get any better than this.

There is a good grassy area for picnics and shade, and the water is not too cold (we swam in June, so it's not like many of the glacier-fed lakes inland). There are also playgrounds in the park, and a number of large grassy areas, such as a wonderful open space close to campsite A19 at Alouette Campground that is ideal for ball games. Maple Ridge has an excellent water park and playground at the entrance to Golden Ears Provincial Park. It is one of the best water parks we have visited and opens at 9:00 a.m. So, if it is hot and the young ones are up with the larks, take them here and exhaust them (the gas station a short walk away sells coffee).

Rainy-day activities

My first trip to Golden Ears was in 1995. It rained. We had no food, two bottles of red wine, no children, and $50.00. We arrived at 11:00 a.m., walked for an hour, got soaked, put up the tent, drank the wine, went to bed for the afternoon, went to the pub, spent all the money, returned to the tent, and went to sleep as the rain continued to pour. We went home after spending 19 hours out of 24 in the tent ... I did not realize until I had kids just how fantastic that time was. If it rains while you're in a tent at Golden Ears, remember that the Lower Mainland with all its attractions is close at hand. Maple Ridge has cinemas, pools, fast-food restaurants, and—in the worst case scenario—home is probably not too far away.

Summary

If you reside in the Lower Mainland and have children who ask, "Are we there yet?" after less than 10 minutes in a vehicle, Golden Ears is the ideal camping spot for you. With boating, swimming, walking, and cycling opportunities here, the whole team will stay entertained. As mentioned above, the biggest advantage to Golden Ears is that it offers easy hiking into the coastal mountains, a good beach with safe, warm waters, and the luxury of civilization only a short drive away. The biggest disadvantage is its popularity. Before the reservation system was in place, I heard of a man who regularly drove from his home in North Vancouver on Wednesdays to book a camping spot for his family for the following five days. Then he would drive back home, leaving the spot vacant until Friday, when he headed out to the park again with his family. My problem with the park is with its popularity and, consequently, the noise that may not die down at 11:00 p.m., as it should. However, if you have never camped before, live in the Lower Mainland, and want to just try one or two nights away, Golden Ears is a good place to start.

Sasquatch Provincial Park

Any first-time visitor to this provincial park cannot help but be in awe of the area's stunning scenery. As you travel the final stretch from Harrison Hot Springs to the gates of the campground, the paved road twists and turns along the edge of Harrison Lake and offers a stunning vista. When we last camped here in July 2003, it was warm when we arrived at Lakeside Campground and we all managed a swim in Deer Lake. We had the lake to ourselves, as we were the only ones in the water. Floating on your back, staring up at the blue skies in the middle of the lake surrounded by high, forested mountains is truly magical. Upon arrival, make sure you and the kids keep an eye out for the mythical Sasquatch, also known as Bigfoot, which is reputed to prowl around the mountains and valleys of the area.

History

The name "Sasquatch" is an English corruption of the Coast Salish word Sasqac. The *Sasqac* is a mythical creature, half man and half beast, which should be avoided. Local Aboriginal bands still report sightings of the Sasquatch around Harrison River, so be warned!

The area is famous for its hot springs, and Harrison Hot Springs calls itself "The Spa of Canada." The Coast Salish people first revered the therapeutic waters as a healing place. Europeans discovered them in 1859 when a pioneer fell out of his canoe into Harrison Lake, and instead of perishing in cold waters, found the lake to be warm. Development started in 1885 when a hotel and bathhouse were built. The water rights to the hot mineral waters are still held by the Harrison Hot Springs Hotel.

Harrison Lake is over 60 kilometres long, making it the largest body of fresh water in southwestern B.C.; the glaciers of the Coast Mountains, north of Pemberton, melt into it. In the 1850s it was on the gold rush route for prospectors travelling between the Fraser River and the goldfields in the Cariboo. At the end of the 19th century, logging started around the lake and is still the main local industry. Huge logging trucks are a regular feature on the roads. Today, Harrison Hot Springs attracts thousands of tourists throughout the year, but somehow manages to retain a quaint village atmosphere.

Swimming is delightful in Sasquatch Provincial Park.

Location

It is easy to see why this park is such a popular family location: it contains four pristine lakes, including the freshwater fjord of massive Harrison Lake, and over 1,220 hectares of land. It is a vast expanse to explore in the midst of beautiful mountain scenery. Sasquatch Provincial Park is located 6 kilometres north of Harrison Hot Springs. Take Highway 9 from the junction of Highway 7 to Harrison Hot Springs (6.5 kilometres), and then take Rockwell Drive to the park entrance. A good gravel road leads into the park and to the campgrounds, 5 kilometres from the park gate. Watch out for logging trucks.

Facilities

In many respects, Sasquatch is not one provincial park but three, as there are three campgrounds here, all quite separate from each other, offering a total of 177 spaces. Of the three, Hicks Lake campground would be my third choice, as the camping spots are smaller than the ones found in most B.C. parks and some are very close together and confined (spaces 18, 19, and 20, for example, are more like parking spaces than camping spots). Bench Campground is near Deer Lake, although it does not have direct access to the lake. The spots are well

Andrew, Jayne, Sam, and Jack look out the front door of their tent.

Jack and Sam enjoy a marshmallow in the great outdoors.

The boys learn how to work a water pump.

The fishing's good at Deer Lake in Sasquatch Provincial Park.

Harrison Lake is one of four in Sasquatch Provincial Park.

Pes?ta Trail, Naikoon, 5 months pregnant. (sorry could not read her writing with trail name

The boys build a driftwood fort on Rathtrevor Beach.

A whale hovers peacefully at Rathtrevor's Nature House.

Miracle Beach Provincial Park is one of the few that still offer interpretive programs.

It's easy to see why kids love Miracle Beach.

These beachcombers try their luck on Miracle Beach.

A construction project on Miracle Beach keeps the boys busy.

Visitors to Alice Lake have a good chance of spotting bald eagles. This excellent lakeside beach is perfect for kids. There's never a dull moment at Alice Lake.

Check out the West Coast Railway Heritage Park in Squamish, near Alice Lake.

Luckily, this bear at Manning Park is just a carving.

Wild alpine flowers abound on the Heather Trail in Manning.

Toe-biters don't stand a chance against these fishermen at Bromley Rock Provincial Park.

Ellison Provincial Park is one of the best campgrounds in the Okanagan.

situated in a forested area, and there are a number of double spots. Be advised that there is little chance of the sun breaking through, as these sites are heavily shaded by trees. My favourite campground at Sasquatch is Lakeside, where a number of spots have direct access onto the lake (try 28, 31, or 32). Even if you are not fortunate enough to obtain one of these perfect sites, all the others at this location are large and in a forested area—great for kids.

All three campgrounds have pit toilets, water pumps, and there is a sani-station but no showers. The campgrounds are not wheelchair accessible. The park accepts reservations and is very popular in the peak summer months. Services available in Harrison Hot Springs include a number of restaurants, pizza parlours, ice cream stores, coffee bars (the one at the Harrison Hot Springs Hotel opens around 6:30 a.m.—ideal if that's the time your baby is awake), shops, and boutiques.

Recreational activities

Hiking

There are two trails located near Hicks Lake. One is a 4-kilometre hike around the lake. This trail may be muddy if the weather has been wet, but otherwise it is an ideal family hike. The other, Beaver Lodge Trail, is an easy 20-minute stroll around a small lake with a beaver lodge. Interpretative boards have been placed along the trail to explain the beavers' habitat and the fish spawning process. Lakeside Trail at Deer Lake is an easy, short walk to a lookout where you might see mountain goats on the nearby bluffs.

Boating

The four lakes at this location (Harrison, Hicks, Deer, and Trout) vary in size and in the recreational pursuits they offer. Harrison and Hicks permit powerboats, while at Deer Lake only electric motors are allowed. Powerboats are also prohibited at Trout Lake, and consequently, it is ideal for canoeing and kayaking. Boaters should be careful of deadheads and of the winds that often come up on the larger lakes. Canoe rentals are available at Hicks and Deer Lake.

Cycling

The gravel roads that lead to the three camping locations are ideal for mountain biking, and the roads and trails in all campgrounds are safe for children to cycle around.

Sasquatch is a real gem for fishing and boating.

Fishing

Trout fishing is reputed to be excellent, and you might also catch kokanee in the lakes. In addition to lake fishing, you can try your luck in the waters of the Harrison and Fraser rivers. Little toe-biters can easily be caught with nets in Deer Lake.

Family activities

With four lakes to choose from, swimming here is delightful. Two beach locations at Hicks Lake ensure sun-worshipping opportunities; one is at the southern end and one is by the group camping area. From this second location it is possible to swim to two small, forested islands that are ideal for exploring. There is a small beach and large grassy area leading to the waters of Deer Lake and also a jetty to sunbathe on. Be warned that the grass near the swimming beaches can be well speckled with the evidence of Canada geese. The day-use area in the park on Harrison Lake has a wonderful beach, a grassy picnic area, and changing facilities, but the waters of the lake are considerably colder than those of Deer Lake. More adventurous campers can windsurf, water ski, or jet ski. The lagoon pool in the town of Harrison Hot Springs has a sandy beach and playground on the beach, which my kids really liked. A play area for children is located at the Lakeside Campground. The town is famous for its mineral pools and for its annual sand sculpture contest in September (see next topic).

Rainy-day activities

The quaint community of Harrison Hot Springs is a lovely place to wander about. There is a beach, and you can arrange excursions on the lake through the summer months. A lakeside trail starting from Harrison Hot Springs Hotel takes you to a structure housing the emerging hot springs; you can put your hand in and feel the warm water. The building is dilapidated, so do not expect a photo opportunity. To truly experience the therapeutic waters, you must book into the Harrison Hot Springs Hotel, or visit the local swimming pool (the cheaper alternative). The pool is also a good place to take a hot shower if you and your offspring have not felt warm water for a few days. The public pool rents lockers, towels, and swimsuits, and is open seven days a week. I advise anyone who has not experienced hot pools to try them, but don't expect to want to do much afterwards other than sleep; they have a very soporific effect.

Each year Harrison Hot Springs holds a sand sculpture competition, with entrants from all over the world. Sand sculptures in the shape of Elvis, castles, loggers, mythical creatures, and more are on show from mid-September until mid-October. In July, Harrison Hot Springs has an annual festival of the arts that includes craft sales and free concerts.

Summary

Sasquatch is a super place for family camping and is a provincial park where, if the weather is good, it is easy to spend a week's vacation. Although there are not a lot of hiking trails, if your family enjoys swimming, sunbathing, fishing, boating, or just having fun surrounded by amazing scenery, then Sasquatch is a real gem. Its easy access to the town of Harrison Hot Springs means campers should not be at a loss for things to do, even if the weather is bad, and there are a lot of places to choose from for eating out. Though it may be cold in the tent, the knowledge that hot mineral pools are only a 20-minute drive away will keep all visitors, whatever their age, happy relaxed campers. In addition, because Sasquatch is a little further away than Alice Lake or Golden Ears, it is not so popular and therefore more likely to have an available space. If the weather report on Wednesday says there's going to be good weather over the weekend, you'll probably be able to reserve a space—even in July and August.

Manning Provincial Park

Unlike many of Vancouver Island's provincial parks, which open in April with a season extending until October, summer activities in Manning are confined to the period between the end of May and September. I once stayed here during the Victoria Day weekend in late May, when cross-country skiing and snowshoeing were the most popular activities and only one trail was open for hiking. If you are planning a trip to this park early in the season, you may want to telephone the visitor centre to determine which facilities are open. While the sun could be shining in Vancouver, the snow may not have thawed here. Having said that, it is a huge park with so many activities and services that even if you have to abandon the tent for a room at the lodge, you and the kids are bound to have fun and find plenty to do.

History

Manning Park is named after E.C. Manning, chief forester of British Columbia from 1936 to 1941. It developed from the Three Brothers Mountain Reserve, created in 1931 to save the alpine meadows from overgrazing by mountain sheep. When the Hope-Princeton Highway opened to the public in 1945, Manning became a popular vacation spot with residents of the Lower Mainland and remains so today. It frequently ranks as the second most popular campground in the province (after Golden Ears). Its history dates back to the First Nations people, who visited the area to hunt and fish; the present Skyline Trail was a well-used route for these early residents.

Location

The park covers over 65,000 hectares within the Cascade Mountains and encompasses two major river systems: the Skagit, which flows to the Pacific Ocean, and the Similkameen, which joins the Okanagan River to the east. The main park administrative centre is between Hope and Princeton. The park itself is within a three hours' drive from Vancouver (224 kilometres) and is located on Highway 3, 30 kilometres east of Hope. If you are travelling to Manning by car from Vancouver, take the more northerly Route 7 instead of Route 1, as it is a far more scenic drive. Kilby is an ideal spot to break the journey because it's about midway between Vancouver and Manning, and it includes a small farm, café, shop, and restored general store dating back to the 1920s. The Kilby Historic Store features not only a cornucopia of long-forgotten items on all of the shelves, but also a downstairs store where children can use period weigh scales, a crank telephone, and an apple press.

Facilities

There are four main campgrounds in Manning Park with a total of 355 camping spaces: Hampton (99); Mule Deer (49); Coldspring (64); and Lightning Lake (143). All spaces at Lightning Lake are reservable, which means campers arriving without reservations are restricted to the other three campgrounds if Lightning Lake is full. Lightning Lake is the only campground with showers and flush toilets and is close to the beach, so it is the preferred camping location if you have young ones to entertain or if you require the luxury of showers. A sani-station is located near the visitor centre ($2.00 fee). All the camping spots in the four campgrounds are large and private, in a well-forested environment. Some sites at Coldspring and Mule Deer are near the river. Unfortunately, traffic noise is audible at Mule Deer, Coldspring, and Hampton, but the traffic isn't heavy during the evening or night.

Manning Park Lodge provides lodge rooms, cabins, chalets, a licensed restaurant, a pub, a coffee bar, and a shop that sells a range of provisions for the camper. It also rents mountain bikes, canoes, kayaks, rowboats, snowshoes, and skis. When I visited, the lodge offered to

The boys have fun with Dad in the playground at Manning Park.

reimburse anyone who, after paying a camping fee, decided to take a break from camping and opt to stay at the lodge—something to bear in mind if the rain starts pouring. The lodge also offers tennis courts, hot tub, dry and wet sauna, and an exercise room; kids under 12 stay free if sharing a room with an adult.

Recreational activities

Hiking

The first port of call for anyone visiting Manning should be the visitor centre, a kilometre east of Manning Park Lodge, to collect a detailed map of the area and to see the displays of stuffed animals and birds. Manning is a true hiker's paradise with over 276 kilometres of trails. There are self-guided nature trails, short easy walks ideal for younger kids (Engineers Loop, Rain Orchid, Twenty Minute Lake, Strawberry Flats, Dry Ridge, Viewpoint Trail), and much longer hikes. One of the most popular longer hikes is the Skyline Trail, which follows the north ridge to Lightning Lake with an elevation gain of 460 metres. For those who like a long walk without the uphill climb, Lightning Lake Chain Trail is an easy 24-kilometre hike along the sides of four lakes. When I last did this walk, hiking with an eight-month-old on my back, I saw deer, beaver, and grouse. Hiking the 21-kilometre Heather Trail in July and August is well worth the effort, as an array of over a hundred species of wild alpine flowers bloom in what BC Parks describes as "a floral carpet more than 24 kilometres in length and up to 5 kilometres in width." One advantage of this trail is that because you drive to the top of a mountain to access it, you have ample energy to marvel at the views. I adore this walk and cannot recommend it too highly. The photographic opportunities are second to none.

Dad hikes with eight-month old Jack.

Horseback riding

You can rent horses (250-840-8844) at Manning Park Corral and explore the four horse trails that range from 20 to 80 kilometres return. Horses are not allowed on the hiking trails. As well as guided trail rides, the park also has pony rides, a small petting zoo, and a teepee for kids to explore.

Boating

Powerboats are prohibited in the park. Canoeing is a joy at Lightning Lake, where there is a launch for car-top boats in the day-use area. As mentioned above, kayaks, canoes, and rowboats can be rented from the Lodge shop and, during the peak months of July and August, from Lightning Lake day-use area ($13.00 per hour, $44.00 per day—2003 prices).

Cycling

You can rent standard mountain bikes and front suspension bikes from the boathouse at Lightning Lake ($11.35 per hour). Mountain bikes are permitted on the 14-kilometre Windy Joe Trail and the 32-kilometre Monument 83 Trail.

Fishing

Anglers can fish for Dolly Varden or rainbow and cutthroat trout in the Similkameen and Sumallo rivers, while fly casters can try for rainbow trout in Lightning and Strike lakes. Fishing licences are available at the front desk of Manning Park Lodge and tackle can be purchased from the resort store.

Wildlife observation

A wide variety of wildlife lives within the park, including over 190 different species of birds, which makes the area popular with ornithologists. It is not unusual to see black bears at the side of the road in the springtime. Although a number of people are somewhat uneasy about sharing Manning Park with the resident bears, it should be noted that there has never been a bear attack in over 50 years of the park's existence.

Family activities

Displays of the area's human and natural history are in the visitor centre, along with an abundance of other information. There is a small play area for children next to Manning Park Lodge with a huge bear sculpture. This is also the place to chase hordes of ground squirrels back into their holes—an activity sure to exhaust all involved except the creatures themselves. Lightning Lake has a beach and safe swimming area, hence the benefit of staying at this campground and not the others. Indeed, many families seem to never leave this location.

If you plan to be at Manning during early August, you are in for a treat. The park invites visitors to make floating lanterns, which they then cast out onto the waters of Lightning Lake at night. This family-oriented affair regularly attracts hundreds of spectators and lantern-makers and creates a magical ambience on the lake. Call the visitor centre (250-840-8836) for the date of this event, which is different every year. Special events also occur on Canada Day; remember to reserve your space well in advance if you want to take part.

Rainy-day activities

The two towns on either side of Manning Park both have something to offer the visitor. Hope promotes itself as the "Chainsaw Capital of the World," and has a rapidly expanding number of chainsaw statues. It has a small museum and is a pleasant river town with all amenities, a good playground in the centre of town, and a McDonald's restaurant with play space. When you travel from Manning to Hope, be sure to stop at the Hope Slide. A plaque and viewpoint indicate the area where, in January 1965, a side of Johnson Peak plunged into the valley, covering the highway with 45 metres of rubble. Also near Hope and not to be missed are the Kettle Valley Railway tunnels. This is an impressive series of five large tunnels that were cut through the granite walls of the Coquihalla Canyon. Named after Shakespearean characters, they last saw railway traffic in 1959, and in 1986 were opened by the provincial parks ministry as the Coquihalla Canyon Recreational Area. Visitors now walk through these tunnels to the sound of roaring waters below. The tunnels are signposted from the Coquihalla Highway and are well worth a visit. Remember to bring a flashlight and a camera.

Princeton lies 134 kilometres from Hope on the other side of Manning Park. Originally settled as a gold-rush town, it has a small museum displaying pioneer artifacts and a riverside playground off the highway that is good for picnics.

Summary

Because Manning is such a large park, it never feels crowded in spite of its high level of use. It's a great place to holiday with your family because you can hike one day, canoe the next, ride a pony the next, and, if you still have energy, ride a mountain bike, swim, and chase ground squirrels. I also particularly appreciate the facilities it offers. On those cold, wet mornings when you wake up and can't face the task of trying to make a fire with wood sodden by last night's rain, it is a real comfort to know that hot coffee and a cooked breakfast can be had, at a reasonable price, only a few kilometres away at the lodge. The washroom facilities also add a level of comfort, of course. While this may not accord with the true camping spirit, even a seasoned camper can appreciate some luxury from time to time.

My little moose-men sport Jerry's Rangers antlers.

VANCOUVER ISLAND AND THE GULF ISLANDS

The following chapter describes three provincial park campgrounds on Vancouver Island—Gordon Bay, Rathtrevor, and Miracle Beach—and one on Galiano Island called Montague Harbour. A number of other provincial parks could have been selected, such as Bamberton, just a 30-minute drive north of Victoria; Englishman River Falls, 13 kilometres south of Parksville; French Beach, 20 kilometres west of Sooke; Little Qualicum Falls, about a 20-minute drive west of Parksville; Ruckle on Saltspring Island; Strathcona, B.C.'s oldest provincial park southwest of Campbell River; as well as Pacific Rim National Park on the west coast of Vancouver Island.

Gordon Bay's location is perhaps the warmest of any campground in Canada; here the camping season starts early and lasts the longest. I have chosen to feature it for this reason, and also because of its wonderful beach. Rathtrevor Beach was selected because of its huge, sandy beach, proximity to Parksville, and fantastic sites, while Miracle Beach is a great size and has tons for a family to do. The final selection is Montague Harbour on Galiano Island. Travelling here involves at least one ferry ride, which is entertaining for any child, and although the campground does not have a huge number of camping spaces, it is a magical place to camp.

Gordon Bay Provincial Park

McDonald, French Beach, Bamberton, Goldstream, and Gordon Bay are all beautiful campgrounds not too far from the main population centres of southern Vancouver Island and are relatively close to each other, which makes picking one over another a difficult decision. Gordon Bay is probably the best family campground, as it offers something for every age group, has excellent facilities, is only a short distance from a picturesque community, and yet is remote enough to have that get-away-from-it-all feel. There can be no better place for sun lovers, as Gordon Bay Provincial Park's 49 hectares are located in one of the warmest valleys on Vancouver Island. The mountains pressing close around Cowichan Lake produce a heat trap that ensures the highest average daily temperature in Canada. The waters of Lake Cowichan offer relief from this heat, as do the shady camping spots.

History

The area has a rich logging history, evident on the mountain slopes surrounding the valley. Logging, still a major industry here today, started in the 1880s, when oxen were used to haul felled wood. The

The main attraction at Gordon Bay is swimming in the weed-free waters of Lake Cowichan.

area was also mined for copper, and the remains of the copper mine can be seen from the well-maintained logging road that rings the lake. The community of Honeymoon Bay, adjacent to the campground, is named after two early settlers, Henry and Edith March, who spent their honeymoon here. Prior to the immigration of European settlers, Coast Salish people lived here, hunting and fishing in the region.

Location

Gordon Bay Provincial Park is on the southern shore of Lake Cowichan, 35 kilometres west of Duncan, 14 kilometres west of the town of Lake Cowichan, and 2 kilometres from the small community of Honeymoon Bay. You can get to it by taking Highway 18, just north of Duncan.

Facilities

Situated in an area of second-growth Douglas fir, this campground has 130 large, nicely laid-out camping spots. Those numbered 1 to 14 are closest to the bay and are separated from the main camping area (and the showers) by a quiet road. If you want to be near the waters of the lake and do not mind a walk to the showers, these are the better sites. There are flush and pit toilets, a sani-station, two shower buildings, and full disabled access. All spots are gravel, large enough to accommodate every type of recreational vehicle, and there are a number of double spots. Reservations are accepted and advisable, as this campground can get very full.

The nearby community of Lake Cowichan has restaurants, accommodation, food stores, gas, a pub, and most amenities. Honeymoon Bay, just a couple of kilometres from the campground, has a good general store that sells camping supplies, candy, pop, ice cream, and in 2003, excellent homemade sausage rolls.

Recreational activities

Hiking

A number of trails lead through the park over a forest floor covered with thimbleberry, salal, salmonberry, and, in the spring, wonderful wildflowers. (Remember, picking vegetation in B.C. parks is prohibited.) The Point Trail leads from the beach to an area of rock overlooking the lake. You can swim here, away from the crowds. Interpretative signs along the route explain the plant life in the area. It takes about 30 minutes to complete this hike. Another trail, which takes two hours to complete, leads from the parking area, through some yellow gates, and past a small lake onto the logging road that rims the lake. You wind up at a viewpoint from which the full beauty of Lake Cowichan can be appreciated.

Boating

There is a boat launch in the park, and waterskiing is permitted on the lake. Lake Cowichan, one of Vancouver Island's largest lakes, is 32 kilometres long and 3 kilometres wide, with plenty of room for powerboaters, jet skiers, canoers, kayakers, and windsurfers. Boats can be rented in Honeymoon Bay.

Cycling

The paved roads of the campground allow pleasant, safe cycling excursions for the young. Numerous logging roads nearby make mountain biking a good alternative for older kids. Also, it is an easy bicycle ride on a quiet road from the campground to the ice cream store at Honeymoon Bay, an ideal early evening activity.

Fishing

The fishing here is reputed to be excellent, as the lake has Dolly Varden, rainbow and cutthroat trout, chum, coho, and spring salmon for the angler. Fishing supplies are available in Honeymoon Bay. Sticklebacks and other small fry can be caught in nets from the beach.

Bicycles rest while campers enjoy the playground.

Bikes are a great way to get around in Gordon Bay Provincial Park.

Family activities

The biggest attraction here is undoubtedly the wonderful sandy/pebbly beach, and large swimming area devoid of weeds and sharp stones. It is difficult to find a more perfect lakeside beach, and although the waters may feel cold at first, they provide a respite from the hot temperatures often experienced here. The swimming area is cordoned off by log booms, which children love to balance on and dive from.

There are numerous picnic tables on a grassy area adjacent to the beach. Many are under the shade of the trees, but you will need to arrive early if you want to reserve one. An adventure playground has been constructed within the camping area, and interpretative programs take place during the summer. Just a short bike ride away in Honeymoon Bay there is also a wonderful playground, which has all the usual climbing equipment as well as basketball nets (and a basketball) and hockey nets on a paved court. For those with older offspring, or access to babysitting for the young ones, there is an attractive nine-hole golf course at Honeymoon Bay, which also has a small restaurant overlooking the greens.

Rainy-day activities

After you've enjoyed the beauty of the park, you can partake in the activities available in the surrounding area. A small museum at Saywell Park in the town of Lake Cowichan offers details about the local history.

Those who want a broader picture can take a tour of the Lake Cowichan Earth Satellite station. The Cowichan River meanders through the community, and it is possible to fish for trout in its waters. An old wooden railway bridge is a novel way to cross the river.

The town of Duncan calls itself the "City of Totems" with over 80 totem poles throughout the town; follow the painted footsteps for a tour. Duncan is also home to the world's largest hockey stick. Just north of Duncan, the smaller, seaside community of Chemainus bills itself as the world's largest outdoor gallery, with over 34 murals and 12 sculptures. Chemainus is very kid friendly (if you avoid the craft and gift shops, which tend to be too full of breakable objects for my comfort), with two playgrounds, numerous ice cream stores and coffee bars, a large water wheel, and, in the summer, horse-drawn carriage rides. With all the murals to see in town, it's a great place to wander around.

Summary

Gordon Bay is a delightful, family-oriented camping location equipped with all amenities, but be warned: it is one of the most popular campgrounds on southern Vancouver Island and is frequently full. I first stayed here mid-week in early June, when only half of the camping spots were open and the BC Parks workers were just gearing up for the peak season. At this time, my partner and I shared the beach with three other couples. We could see only two boats on the lake, and were the only people brave enough to swim in the cold waters. It was tranquil; it was beautiful; it was special. This experience was in sharp contrast to my last attempt to enjoy the facilities of Gordon Bay one weekday in August with my three- and four-year-olds. Five years after my initial visit, it was noisy; it was busy; it was stressful—but it was ideal for kids. Gordon Bay merits its reputation as one of the most popular family camping spots on Vancouver Island.

Rathtrevor Beach Provincial Park

With over 160,000 visitors per year, this is Vancouver Island's most popular provincial park and one of the most popular in the province. Within the camping fraternity, stories circulate of the impossibility of finding a camping spot here in July and August, with lines of RVs waiting to get in. Anyone who has seen the 2,000 metres of beach and the first-rate camping facilities, including some of the largest, most private camping spots on the BC Parks roster, can easily understand its popularity. Rathtrevor is probably the perfect location—if the weather co-operates—for a family vacation.

History

Rathtrevor got its name from a gold prospector and pioneer, William Rath, who settled in the area with his wife and family in 1886. He died in 1903, leaving his wife with the farm and five children. To supplement her farming income she started to charge visitors for picnicking on her land. Soon picnicking led to camping and she charged a fee of 25 cents, then 50 cents per weekend (at press time the camping fee was $22.00 per night). Mrs. Rath eventually developed the land into a full campground and added the word "trevor" to the name for effect. BC Parks acquired Rathtrevor in 1967. The park started with 140 spots and four large parking areas and was expanded to 174 spaces in 1976. The visitor centre is located in the old family farmhouse.

Location

Rathtrevor Beach encompasses more than 347 hectares of land (including 2 kilometres of sandy shoreline) and is situated on Highway 19A, 2 kilometres south of Parksville (29 kilometres north of Nanaimo). It has views of the Strait of Georgia and the Coast Mountains on the mainland beyond. Interpretative boards located on the beach identify peaks in this mountain range, so you do not have to guess.

Facilities

It is not only the sea and sand that attract campers to this location. I believe the camping spots themselves are some of the best in the province. The 175 spacious sites are located in a forest of Douglas fir and accommodate every type of recreational vehicle. There are a number of double spots, and group camping is also available. The vegetation is quite dense, affording privacy from even the nearest neighbour. The campground is fully equipped with a sani-station, showers, flush and pit toilets, and wheelchair accessibility. The washrooms are tiled and have baby changing facilities. A maze of paved roads with names such as Foam Flower Lane and Sea Blush Lane provides access to the sites. Reservations are accepted and advisable as the campground is *very* popular, especially during the months of July and August. Services are available in Parksville. In 2003, a small concession at the visitor centre sold ice cream, pop, candy bars, chips, coffee, and toys, and I understand that there are plans to expand this service in the future.

Recreational activities

Hiking

There are over 4 kilometres of easy hiking trails in the park, leading through the wooded area and along the shore. There are also self-guided nature trails. Some trails are closed to cyclists. One of the best pastimes we found was beachcombing along the beach at low tide. There is also a trail, which runs parallel to the day-use area and is a good place to people-watch.

Boating

You can windsurf and canoe here, but there is no boat launch.

Cycling

Children adore this location for cycling. The paved roads in the camping area and the many trails and quiet roads in the park are a safe cycling haven to explore. The paved roads are also a delight for rollerblading. In 2003, the campground administrators started to rent tandem bikes for use in the park and have plans to expand this service in 2004.

Wildlife observation

Bird watching is reputed to be good in the springtime and during the annual herring spawn.

Family activities

Famed for its beautiful sandy shingle leading to warm, clear waters, Rathtrevor is "unbeatable for swimming," according to BC Parks literature. This is the perfect family beach campground for picnicking and playing in the safe waters. Many families spend a week or longer just on the beach, which is well equipped with fresh water, a change house, and picnic tables. Dogs are prohibited on the beach. If you want to escape the crowds, you can find your own private beach spot on the waterfront closer to the campground, where there are more rocks and logs, but fewer people and less noise. Lots of washed-up logs in these more remote places are great places to build dens and play pirate games.

There are two children's play areas. In summer months, an amphitheatre is used to deliver visitor programs like "Freddy the Frog," "Critter Olympics," and "Bee Social." The visitor centre, open 11:00 a.m. to 4:00 p.m. during the summer, has a first-class display of natural and human history artifacts, including a display of live bees, stuffed birds (including bald eagles, owls, and hawks), photographs showing the park's development and the logging history of the region, and marine life presentations. Staff members at this centre are keen to provide information about the animals and plants found in the park, in addition to offering advice on a multitude of other park-related issues. Jerry's Rangers programs for kids are offered during the summer months for a $1.00 fee.

Rainy-day activities

There are a number of commercial facilities that have sprung up near the park. These include mini-golf, go-carts, boat rentals, golf courses, water parks, and adventure playgrounds. The neighbouring community

The visitor centre at Rathtrevor Beach Provincial Park is located in an old family farmhouse.

Sea, sand, and plenty of driftwood attract campers to Rathtrevor Beach.

of Parksville is named after Nelson Park, one of the first settlers in the area, and has a street full of restaurants and fast-food outlets. It also boasts a small museum and one of the Island's oldest churches, St. Anne's Anglican Church, built in 1894.

Summary

This campground is extremely popular. However, if you arrive to find it full, you do not have far to travel to find alternative provincial park camping. Englishman River Falls Provincial Park is only 13 kilometres away, and Little Qualicum Falls is 24 kilometres from Rathtrevor. Although Rathtrevor is extremely busy, the number of people employed to administer the park's facilities ensures that amenities are well cared for. While the camper relaxes on the beach, a platoon of workers empties the garbage, cleans bathrooms, rakes the gravel, and provides every type of help and assistance.

The fact that the new parks administrators have decided to continue offering the Jerry's Rangers kids' programs and the adult-oriented interpretive programs, and that they plan to expand school-based services such as field trips as well, suggests Rathtrevor Beach will retain its reputation as one of the best places to camp, or just visit, with kids in B.C.

Miracle Beach Provincial Park

With its wide, sandy beach and views across the Strait of Georgia to the Coast Mountains, it is easy to see why this campground is attractive to both adults and children, providing an ideal spot for a family beach vacation. We last stayed here in August 2003, and I was delighted to learn that services that had been cut from many other provincial parks remained here, including the campground hosts, the Jerry's Rangers programs for kids, and interpretive programs (albeit for a $1.00 fee). Every Thursday, Friday, Saturday, and Sunday in the summer, presentations such as "Bonkers for Bats" and "Otter Wise" were taking place in the nature house or amphitheatre. This really is a kids' place to camp.

History

The area has been inhabited for millions of years. In 1988, fossilized remains of a dinosaur were found just south of the park. These remains of an *Elasmosaur*, a swimming reptile that measured four metres in length, are believed to be 800 million years old. The discovery was the most significant dinosaur find this side of the Rockies. European immigrants began to populate the area at the beginning of the 20th century. They recognized its immense farming, mining, and fishing potential. One of the profitable fishing streams was Black Creek, which runs through the park. Miracle Beach allegedly got its name because two severe fires, which devastated much of the surrounding forest, narrowly missed it.

Location

The 135-hectare Miracle Beach Provincial Park is adjacent to Elma Bay on the sheltered shores of the east coast of Vancouver Island, 131 kilometres north of Nanaimo and midway between Courtenay and Campbell River. It is situated just off Highway 19; a paved access road carries you the 2 kilometres from the highway to the campground entrance. There are views of the Coast Mountains, and interpretative boards on the beach depict and identify the visible peaks, many of which are named after early European explorers.

Facilities

Miracle Beach has 193 large, private camping spots in a second-growth forest of Douglas fir, hemlock, and western red cedar. In most campgrounds there are a few less desirable spots, but not here. These camping spaces are among the best BC Parks offers, and the trees make them truly private. Paved and gravel roads—named after the trees growing in the park—wind through the campground, and it is only a five-minute stroll from your tent to the beach. All amenities are here, including showers, flush and pit toilets, a sani-station, and disabled access. Reservations are accepted and advised if you want to camp in the peak of summer. There is a small concession in the nature house selling ice cream, candy bars, and a few toys.

Views of the Coast Mountains across the Strait of Georgia are spectacular from Miracle Beach.

Recreational activities

Hiking

There are a few walking trails, an interpretative trail, and a dog-walking trail in the park, but the total is less than 5 kilometres. However, the oceanfront is wonderful to wander along.

Cycling

The paved roads of the campground, together with the trails, create a safe environment for even the smallest cyclist. When I last visited, cycling was a popular pastime for every age group. A number of paved roads make rollerblading another option.

Fishing

The best fishing is in October, when it is possible to fly cast for coho from the beach mouth at the end of Black Creek. The town of Campbell River claims to be the salmon capital of the world and is a perfect place for the angling enthusiast to spend some time. It is estimated that 60 percent of visitors to Campbell River come for the fishing.

Family activities

Of course, one of the main attractions is the lovely, long sand and pebble beach, perfect for swimming and sunbathing. Numerous logs along the shoreline provide backrests and props where adults can sit and read while the children run off to the safe waters, or as my children did, build forts and pirate ships with the debris. The beach is equipped with a change house, picnic tables, and toilets. Dogs are prohibited. Low tide reveals rock pools to explore, and there is a vast array of small creatures and objects for young and old beachcombers to discover; lift up stones to reveal millions of tiny crabs. There is also a children's playground at the entrance to the campground.

To supplement personal beach and woodland explorations, the excellent visitor centre/nature house has displays of whales, fossils, butterflies, bugs, and snakes. As mentioned above, parks staff are on hand to offer information and provide interpretative programs with appealing names such as "Jerry the Jellyfish" and "Slime Time." The place is a real hive of activity during the summer months. When we visited in 2000, a display featuring a fire-bellied tree frog was billed as "visiting from Australia." The cross-section of a 300-year-old Douglas fir, 1.7 metres in diameter, is on display outside the centre. During the evening, programs for all the family are presented in the park amphitheatre.

There is a caption here: Kids learn about local wildlife at the nature house.

Rainy-day activities

As the park is near two large centres of population (Campbell River, 19 kilometres to the north, and Courtenay, 24 kilometres to the south), there are a number of non-beach-related activities available. These include golfing, ferry trips to the islands of Quadra, Cortes, Hornby, and Denman, and boating and fishing excursions. There is a museum and archive in Courtenay, and to the west of the town is the Puntledge River Hatchery. Courtenay also has a good children's playground, water park, and outdoor swimming pool near the centre of town.

Campbell River has seen considerable redevelopment in recent years and now has a number of shops to visit and oceanfront paths to walk, including one with a fantastic array of wooden statues. There is also a pier where you can rent fishing tackle and purchase ice cream and watch seals. If you must go there, the McDonald's in town has a play space.

Summary

Miracle Beach is not just perfect by day; at night you can see many more stars than you can in the city, and it is wonderful to sit on the beach and watch the sun go down. Although the beach here is not as large as Rathtrevor's to the south, these two campgrounds offer similar facilities, making it difficult to decide which one to select. Miracle Beach is smaller and slightly less developed than Rathtrevor, and is not quite as popular.

Montague Harbour
Provincial Marine Park

Two hours from downtown Vancouver or Victoria, a beautiful little campground waits with everything you need for a weekend escape from the city: calm sea waters, wide white beaches, shady camping spots, and a tranquillity that only an island can provide. I adore this place and camped here when I was eight months pregnant with my second son in August 2000. At this time it was hot, but the shade of the camping spots and sea breeze made it bearable. I swaggered around the campground like a galleon in full sail with my 40-pound bump leading the way, gaining sympathetic looks and comments from all the other campers. In my opinion, Galiano Island is the nicest of the Gulf Islands and a lovely, quiet place to camp.

Here I am, eight months' pregnant and still camping!

History

The island is named after Dionisio Alcala Galiano, commander of the *Sutil*, who explored the area and claimed the island for Spain in 1792. However, shell middens at Montague Harbour, which are estimated to be over 3,000 years old, testify to the much earlier, semi-permanent settlement of the Coast Salish people in the area. There is an archaeological site in the park where spearheads, carvings, and arrows have been found. One of the earliest European settlers on Galiano was a man named Henry Georgeson, who came from the Shetland Islands in the mid-1800s, purchased 59 hectares of land, and hunted deer. The people who settled on the island in the 19th century tended to build their homes at the south end of Galiano, near Whaler Bay, Sturdies Bay, and Georgeson Bay. Most of the island's 1,000 inhabitants still live in this area.

The 20th century saw the development of a fishing industry. Herring was salted in five different places on Galiano; Japanese people ran four of the plants, while the fifth was a Chinese operation. A cannery and saltery were started on the island, but they were closed during the Second World War when the Japanese were interned and sent to the Interior of B.C. Today, many artists and craftspeople have chosen to live here, and there are a few restaurants, craft shops, and a first-rate bakery in the area around Sturdies Bay.

Location

Montague Harbour is B.C.'s oldest marine park. When it opened in 1959, it was the first provincial park to serve visitors who arrived in boats as well as by car or on foot. The park encompasses an 89-hectare area that starts 5 metres below sea level and rises to 180 metres above. It includes a lagoon, a tidal salt marsh, a forest of various types of trees and undergrowth, a beach, cliffs, and rocks, and consequently is a varied and interesting place to explore or relax. If you do not have your own boat, you can reach Galiano Island via BC Ferries from Swartz Bay on Vancouver Island (about 45 minutes) or from Tsawwassen on the mainland (about 50 minutes). Then drive 10 kilometres from Sturdies Bay to the park. During the summer months ferry trips should be reserved (www.bcferries.bc.ca).

Facilities

There are 40 well-positioned camping spots here: 25 are suitable for vehicles and are set in a forested area with Douglas fir, western hemlock, and western red cedar, while many of the 15 walk-in sites overlook the harbour and have better views than the drive-in sites. The drive-in sites are large and accommodate almost all sizes of recreational vehicles. Group camping is also available. Facilities are the basic ones found in BC Parks (pit toilets, water, picnic tables, firepits). There is no sani-station or disabled access. Reservations are accepted and advisable. There are a number of bed and breakfast accommodations, lodges, and cabins on the island. Most services are at Sturdies Bay, including a grocery and general store, restaurants, and a bakery that not only supplies tasty baked goods but is also a great place to sit and drink coffee and watch the world go by. You

The boys bond on the beach.

can rent kayaks and bicycles in the village (including bike trailers for kids). The marina adjacent to the campground has a small store and coffee bar where you can get some basic supplies. When I last stayed at Montague Harbour, this coffee bar served delicious freshly baked cinnamon buns first thing in the morning.

Recreational activities

Hiking

The longest trail takes you around Gray Peninsula, named after Captain Gray, an early explorer who settled on the island and cultivated an orchard that supplied fruit to the people of Victoria. This 3-kilometre trail follows the shoreline and lagoon around the peninsula, which was created by glacial action thousands of years ago. Other little trails zigzag their way around the campsites on the park's north side. Members of the local community have worked to create a number of hiking trails on the island and recommend that tourists visit Bellhouse Provincial Park—described as possibly the most scenic park in the Gulf Islands— and hike to Bluffs Park and Mount Galiano. When we attempted this a few years ago, the signage left a lot to be desired, but the views of Active Pass were worth it. There are also trails along Bodega Ridge at the north end of the island.

Boating

There is a boat launch in the park, and kayaks can be rented from the nearby marina and at Sturdies Bay. Kayaking is a good way to explore the coastal scenery and is safe, as the waters of the bay are generally calm.

Cycling

While there is little opportunity for cycling in the campground itself, Galiano has lovely, quiet roads, especially once you leave the main population centre. Be warned, however, that Galiano is not by any means flat! Bikes can be rented in Sturdies Bay. Cyclists can easily travel the length of the island on Porlier Pass Road. If you are cycling in the summer, you will find ice cream stores and cafés to refresh yourself en route.

Fishing

The area has abundant salmon and shellfish. This feature is not only appreciated by anglers, but also by the population of bald eagles and other birds that frequent the island.

Family activities

This provincial park is suitable for retired individuals with time on their hands and for families. The sandy, shell-covered beaches and the clear, warm waters are perfect for swimming, beachcombing, and sunbathing, while the easy walks and trails within the park's boundaries are alternative attractions. There is a floating nature house in the park, and during the evening, you might find yourself looking through the transparent floor of this structure into the ocean to see the sea life. When we visited, the presenters gave fascinating accounts of the creatures that can be viewed in this magical way. Programs like this are now under review.

Rainy-day activities

Montague Harbour is an ideal base from which to explore other Gulf Islands in your own craft or on BC Ferries. There are daily sailings to Mayne, Pender, Saturna, and Saltspring Islands, and if you have older children who like cycling, trips to the other Gulf Islands make great cycling excursions. Saltspring is the largest Gulf Island, and you can get there by catching a small passenger-only ferry in Sturdies Bay. This ferry is operated by a charming husband-and-wife team; it plies its way between Galiano, Mayne, and Saltspring Islands, and juice is served on the trip. It docks in Ganges, where you will find a good playground a short walk away, numerous craft shops and restaurants to explore, as well as a broad walk around the harbour.

Summary

Galiano is smaller and less commercialized than Saltspring Island, but offers more amenities than Pender, and Montague Harbour is a park that can be appreciated by every age group. While I have attempted to describe the many activities available here, probably the best activity is to unwind and enjoy the beach. As the park is relatively small, the beach is never crowded, and you can spend many hours reading and building sandcastles by the calm waters. In the evening you can view breathtaking sunsets, and at night the heavens explode with an abundance of stars that fill a sky far bigger than what you see in the city. If you need a change from campground food, try the Hummingbird Pub, which has a great outdoors area for kids to explore and excellent food, often accompanied by live entertainment. Be forewarned, though, as this establishment is very popular and has a great reputation, so it can get very busy. You may have to wait awhile for the culinary delights, but it will be worth it.

This Okanagan beach is perfect for building sandcastles.

THE SHUSHAP AND OKANAGAN

Before I had children I did not care much for the Okanagan, regarding it as too populated, too barren, and too hot. How opinions change. Now I like the convenience of the donut shops and the numerous coffee shops and fast-food outlets, love the warm temperatures in the spring and fall, and appreciate the vast array of services on offer. The campgrounds in this section are Shuswap Lake, Ellison, Bear Creek, Okanagan Lake, and Haynes Point. They all vary considerably in size, and all except Shuswap are very near to major centres of population. Shuswap is the furthest north, in the region of B.C. often referred to as the "High Country". However, it is less than two hours from the Okanagan and shares the same fantastic water-based activities and almost-guaranteed gorgeous weather. It is primarily for these reasons that I have selected these parks. Other recommendations for family camping in the Shuswap–Okanagan include Mabel Lake Provincial Park, a little off the beaten track almost an hour's drive southeast of Salmon Arm, on a wonderful lake near the Monashee Mountain Range (and therefore a cooler part of the Okanagan). Fintry, a newer campground is in a fantastic parklike setting approximately 30 kilometres north of Kelowna, and Otter Lake, not far from Princeton, is set amongst some lovely scenery by a beautiful lake.

Shuswap Lake Provincial Park

If you are a camper who primarily enjoys hiking and exploring by land, and if you do not want to be surrounded by the younger generation, then you may decide that Shuswap is *not* the place to be, as this provincial park and its environs are family oriented, dominated by lake- and beach-based activities. However, if you are a camper who loves the water or has little ones to entertain, this is your paradise. Shuswap Lake, with over 1,000 kilometres of waterways that form an unconventional "H" shape, is a real magnet to the boating fraternity in the summer months. At the height of the season 350 houseboats, together with many hundreds of smaller craft, sail the warm waters. But it is not only boaters who flock to its shores. Those with young children are drawn by the kilometre of fine beach and the hot climate that guarantees many days can be lazily spent enjoying the sun, waters, and sand. And for those who just want to spend their time fishing, there is little to stop the pursuit of this pastime.

Shuswap Lake is actually made up of four arms: Shuswap Lake itself, Salmon Arm (connecting to Mara Lake), Anstey Arm, and Seymour Arm, which all meet at Cinnamousun Narrows. The only disadvantage to this water wonderland is that it does get extremely busy, with the main campground operating at capacity in July and August. Fortunately there are a number of campgrounds accessible only by boat, so for those with alternative modes of transport, peace is only a few knots away.

History

Shuswap Lake Provincial Park was created in 1956 and is the largest and most commercialized park in the Shuswap region, offering over 270 spaces. The area is named after the Shuswap people (Secwepemc First Nation), the most northern of the Salishan language group, who were the first to appreciate this extensive inland water system and to enjoy the abundant natural resources. Evidence of these early inhabitants has been found in the form of kekulis—semi-underground pit houses built for enduring the winter—that have been found at Scotch Creek and Herald provincial parks. Pictographs or rock paintings are also in evidence on rock faces around the lake. Europeans arrived throughout the 19th century as fur traders, explorers, and then surveyors—working for the Canadian Pacific Railway—travelled the area. Gold was discovered in the region, which resulted in a flood of population. Towns and settlements rapidly appeared and disappeared as the gold prospectors arrived, worked the find, and moved on. Today little remains of their exploits.

Location

Shuswap Lake Provincial Park is on the lake from which it takes its name, on the old delta of Scotch Creek. The unusual lake formations are the result of glacial action that formed steep valley walls ringed by gently sloping mountainsides. The park is just under 150 hectares in area, and includes Copper Island, 2 kilometres offshore. Part of the reason for Shuswap's popularity is undoubtedly its central location, easily accessible from Highway 1. Ninety kilometres east of Kamloops, at Squilax, turn off the highway onto a 20-kilometre twisting, paved road that leads to the campground. Most supplies can be found at a number of stores close to the entrance of the park, while more extensive supplies are available in Sorrento, 35 kilometres away.

Facilities

Because it is one of B.C.'s largest provincial parks, the facilities offered at Shuswap Lake are comprehensive and include 272 camping spots suitable for every type of recreational vehicle, flush and pit toilets, sani-station, showers, and full disabled access. The camping spots are found in a dense second-growth forest of Douglas fir, aspen, white birch, and western red cedar. Reservations are accepted and strongly advised, as

The boys enjoy a picnic in the park with Dad.

BC Parks says Shuswap Lake operates at full capacity from mid-July to Labour Day. This large provincial park is one of only three located on the lake that offers both vehicle and tent camping. The others are Herald (51 spaces), and Silver Beach (35 spaces). If you find Shuswap full, Silver Beach is the next closest to try. There are also wilderness campgrounds, only accessible by boat, at six locations on the lake.

Recreational activities

Hiking

Shuswap is not a great place for serious hiking. Next to the campground is a small nature trail, and there is a perimeter trail running near the park boundary, but neither takes more than an hour to complete. The perimeter trail had little to commend it, as I found myself walking by a large metal fence for a good portion of the way. There is a 3-kilometre trail on Copper Island that takes hikers to a viewpoint of the lake and area (remember the waterproof camera). During the summer, mule deer inhabit Copper Island. There are also short trails at Roderick Haig-Brown Provincial Park (see "Rainy-day activities").

Cycling

One of the most popular recreational pursuits here is cycling, as there are over 11 kilometres of paved road in the park itself, and a mountain-bike trail has been developed. During the evening hours the park is full of kids on rollerblades and bikes.

A deserted sunny beach provides a great view of Copper Island.

Fishing

The entire Shuswap Lake system is known for good game-fish species including rainbow, lake, and brook trout, kokanee salmon, squawfish, burbot, carp, whitefish, and suckers. The best fishing months are May through June and October through November.

Boating

Water sports are popular here. There is a boat launch, and the waters attract powerboaters, water skiers, canoers, kayakers, windsurfers, jet skiers, and houseboaters. As one would expect, the waters are particularly busy near the campground and where the arms of the lake meet at Cinnamousun Narrows, but as there are four long arms to Shuswap Lake, it does not take too long to escape the crowd. You can rent canoes or kayaks at commercial outlets adjacent to the campground. Unfortunately the dreaded noisy jet ski can also be rented nearby. While there is no overnight boat mooring at Shuswap Lake, nearby Shuswap Lake Provincial Marine Park offers this facility as well as six separate developed and eight undeveloped camping locations along all four arms of the lake.

Family activities

This is a place for family fun, which centres on the kilometre-long beach.

A safe swimming area with beautiful sand, warm water, and two diving platforms is the most popular area of the park from 9:00 a.m. until well into the evening hours. Shuswap Lake has a busy visitor centre, which provides historical information about the area. Shuswap boasts what must be one of the largest and most comprehensive children's play areas of any provincial park, and, as mentioned above, commercial recreational activities (for example, kayak rentals and go-carts) are easily accessible in the surrounding area.

Rainy-day activities

Boaters do not have to be told about the massive expanse of lake and shoreline that is theirs to explore. For those who do not have access to

Mum enjoys a rare moment of peace and solitude.

this mode of transportation, Roderick Haig-Brown Provincial Park, less than 8 kilometres from Shuswap, is an alternative, especially if you plan to visit in September. This park on the Adams River is accessible to the spectacle of a major run of sockeye salmon. The fish return every year, but every four years the river turns red as approximately 1.5 million fish crowd into the area. During these peak years BC Parks arranges a "Salute to the Salmon," with displays and additional staff on hand to describe the event. (The next spectacle occurs in 2006.) Even if your visit does not coincide with this event, it is worth visiting the park to learn of the salmon-spawning process and to walk the trails.

Summary

As mentioned above, this area is extremely popular during the summer months and may not be to everyone's taste at this time, because it presents the more commercial side to camping in B.C. parks. However, if you have children to entertain, Shuswap Lake, with its warm summer days and fantastic beach, comes highly recommended. When we last visited, there seemed to be a number of parents looking after highly contented but energetic children who ran, cycled, played, and made new friends around the campsite. I am sure all these children will grow up remembering the summers of their childhood as always idyllic, and I felt quite jealous of their unadulterated enthusiasm and *joie de vivre*. For those who want to experience the delights of Shuswap Lake from a quieter vantage point, Herald (which caters more to the older camper) and Silver Beach provincial parks provide more tranquil alternatives.

Ellison Provincial Park

Famous for having Canada's only freshwater dive park, Ellison must also rank as one of the best campgrounds in the Okanagan, primarily because it does not feel as busy as many of the others in the region and therefore offers a quieter family camping experience. Although only 16 kilometres away from a major centre of population, it does not suffer from the constant hum of traffic as do other popular parks in the Okanagan do (e.g. Haynes Point, Okanagan Lake). It is nestled in a Douglas fir and ponderosa pine forest on the northeastern shore of Okanagan Lake in one of the warmest areas of the province, which makes it easy to see why campers return here for a week or more at a time. Every age group can enjoy this idyllic spot from April to October. This is the campground that, of all our 2003 camping excursions, my boys most want to return to.

History

This area owes its development to a man named Cornelius O'Keefe, who in the 19th century, while driving cattle from Oregon to the hungry men in the gold-mining areas of the Cariboo, discovered fertile grassland at the north end of Okanagan Lake. He decided not to drive cattle anymore, but to raise them in this location. He built a ranch, which still exists today (see "Rainy-day activities"). In 1962, more than a hundred years after O'Keefe first travelled the area, Ellison Provincial Park was created.

Location

This provincial park is located 16 kilometres south of Vernon on the northeast shore of Okanagan Lake. Signposts in Vernon indicate how to get to Okanagan Landing Road, which takes you to the park. The road from Okanagan Landing follows the lakeside, twisting and turning past orchards, farms, and ranches that have been an integral part of the community for over a century. The park is situated in 200 hectares of forested benchland high above a shoreline of rocks, cliffs, beaches, scenic headlands, and tranquil coves. To the west are the rolling hills of the Thompson Plateau and to the east are the distant Monashee Mountains.

Facilities

The 71 gravel camping spots here are perfect. Some have views of the lake, a few have direct access to the adventure play area (try staying at 71, 69, 66, and 64 for this), and all are spacious and private enough to accommodate even the largest RV. There are flush and pit toilets, water, and wood for sale; there are no showers or a sani-station. The park is wheelchair accessible and reservations are accepted.

Recreational activities

Hiking

Six kilometres of easy, child-friendly hiking trails wind their way through the park. Paved trails, a little steep in places, lead from the campground to the beaches at South Cove and Otter Bay, and a third unpaved trail leads to a pet-friendly beach from campsite number 11. The popular Nature Trail Loop provides a 40-minute walk where explorers may see Columbian ground squirrels and even porcupines, according to BC Parks literature. Interpretive signs are along this route.

Fishing

For those without a boat, it is possible to catch carp, burbot, kokanee, Rocky Mountain whitefish, and large rainbow trout from the shoreline. However, those with access to the waters are the true angling winners. Vernon's tourist board states there are over 100 lakes in which to fish, all less than an hour's drive from the city, with Okanagan Lake being one of the longest.

Boating/Diving

There is no boat launch in the park itself, but there is a public boat launch (signposted from the road) 6 kilometres north of the campground. Waterskiing, powerboating, and the ever-pestering jet skiers are allowed on the lake; mooring buoys are provided in South Bay and Otter Bay. Otter Bay in Ellison is the home of Canada's only freshwater dive park. A number of objects and artifacts have been sunk here to attract fish and rubber-clad individuals. BC Parks says the area has "been enhanced to provide a variety of fish for snorkeling and scuba diving" but seems reluctant to specify how this enhancement has occurred. For those of us who do not wish to try the activity, this is a great place to "diver watch," especially at the end of the day, as night diving is popular. Campers wishing to rent diving equipment should contact Innerspace Dive and Kayak at 3306 32nd Avenue in Vernon at 250-549-2040.

Family activities

The three protected beach areas with soft, peach-coloured sand are ideal places for swimming, sandcastle construction, and sunbathing.

The soft, peach-coloured sand at Ellison Provincial Park is delightful.

A change house with cold, freshwater showers is situated between the two coves, Otter Bay and South Cove. The third swimming location is at Sandy Beach (the only beach that permits animals). The existence of three locations ensures you never feel crowded, even if hordes of Grade 3 schoolchildren arrive, as was the case when we stayed. During our visit, we found that a volleyball net had been set up by Otter Bay. After a busy day swimming and sunbathing, children can find further entertainment in the adventure playground or playing ball games on the manicured playing field. This field has an underground sprinkler system and it looks like it should belong to an expensive Okanagan golf course rather than a B.C. provincial park. This grass is also home to a great many ground squirrels that run around and appear out of dozens of holes, ready to be chased by the overenthusiastic five-year-olds. One of the most popular pursuits is an evening of stargazing, as the clear Okanagan skies offer fantastic astronomical opportunities. The paved roads of the park are good cycling and rollerblading terrain.

Rainy-day activities

The community of Vernon, the oldest town in the province's Interior, dating back to 1892, is only 16 kilometres away and offers many "urban" pursuits. These include a museum and archive, art gallery, golf and mini-golf, waterslides, and leisure centres. At the historic O'Keefe Ranch,

12 kilometres north of Vernon, there are tours of the O'Keefe mansion, preserved and restored heritage buildings (including a picture-postcard church), a huge model railway display, tons of cowboy memorabilia, a picnic area, restaurant, and gift shop. There are also a number of farm animals, adding further authenticity to this 1867 ranch. Should you find babysitters for the kids, the Okanagan Springs Brewery in Vernon offers tours during the summer months.

Summary

Our two boys loved this park, as we were lucky enough to secure a campsite next to the field and playground. First thing in the morning they were up and out, playing with the friends they had made the previous evening. My three-year-old managed to befriend four 13-year-old girls, which was a wonderful babysitting treat for us. While we were free to enjoy the sunshine and a book, he was kept entertained by four

A half-buried Jack gets down to earth.

surrogate mothers, while our four-year-old chased ground squirrels. Unlike many provincial parks that offer good family camping, Ellison is not large. It is very friendly, and in my opinion, offers better swimming than the Okanagan Lake or Haynes Point campgrounds and also has nicer beaches. This is my favourite campground in the Okanagan.

Bear Creek Provincial Park

When I think of Bear Creek I am reminded of one of the most aromatic experiences of my life. I first visited in early spring, on a hot day when the smell of the cottonwood trees, which extend through the campground to the beach, was mingling with the scent of fir and pine to create an aroma that almost made me dizzy. When we visited in late June 2003, my four-year-old commented on the fact it was snowing— the cottonwood trees were shedding their spores to such an extent we even had "snowball" fights.

Smell is not the only draw here. In addition to its aromatic qualities, this is a campground with a friendly feel, ideal for families and campers who want the outdoors experience without travelling too far from the hustle and bustle of life. While Bear Creek is in the busy Okanagan region, it is situated on a relatively quiet road. Although the city of Kelowna is clearly in view, if you look the other way you can pretend it does not exist. Like the other campgrounds in the Okanagan, Bear Creek is extremely popular, so do not expect to find a spot easily in July or August, and consider reserving if you want a holiday here. Do consider visiting even if you do not have a reservation or an intention to camp, as it is a wonderful place for a picnic and walk.

History

The 167-hectare park was created in 1981. Prior to then the S.M. Simpson Company had owned the land, as the shoreline was ideal for "booming," or storing, floating logs. The Simpson Company sold

The steep hiking trail near the gorge at Bear Creek Provincial Park is not recommended for children under five.

Can you see the Ogopogo? Bear Creek Provincial Park on Okanagan Lake is a good place to look for it.

its interest to Crown Zellerbach Canada Ltd., and in 1981 the Devonian Group of Alberta helped the B.C. government purchase the land. Crown Zellerbach retains the right to continue booming, so floating logs, an integral part of the B.C. economy, are often seen in the waters adjacent to the park (and a number of "escaped" logs provide floating fun for children). The quality of the creek's water was recognized many years ago by the Kelowna Brewing Company, which established a brewery nearby. Unfortunately this is no longer in existence, although occasionally old quart-sized beer bottles are found.

Location

Situated in the Central Okanagan Basin, Bear Creek (sometimes called Lambley Creek) is just 9 kilometres west of Kelowna on the western side of Okanagan Lake. You reach it via a paved access road. All services are available in Kelowna.

Facilities

The campground has 122 wonderful private spots. Paved roads ribbon throughout the park, making access easy for even the largest RV. Some

An impromptu game of volleyball beside the lake looks like a lot of fun.

of the sites have views of the bubbling creek, so campers can sleep to the sound of murmuring water; others are beside fantastic grassy areas, ideal for ball games. The campground is fully equipped with showers, flush and pit toilets, and access for the disabled. Reservations are accepted and strongly advised. In 2003 the park administrator established a small concession for the sale of ice cream, candy bars, ice, and pop.

Recreational activities

Hiking

Although not long (a total of only 10 kilometres), the hiking trails around Bear Creek are a delight. Information on the campground notice board states the main Canyon Rim Trail takes one to two hours to complete, although I did it in 40 minutes, including stops for photographs of the lake, waterfalls, and gorge (not really recommended if your children are under 5). It is quite steep in places but worth the effort, with many opportunities to photograph the rushing waters of Bear Creek. Interpretative boards along the route give information on the fauna and flora of the area, and if you are fortunate enough to hike this trail in spring you will see and smell a stunning array of wildflowers. For those with less stamina, the Mid Canyon Trail also grants access to some spectacular views, especially from the aptly named "Steep and Deep Canyon" lookout.

Boating/Fishing

Powerboats are permitted on the lake via the park's boat launch. Canoes, rowboats, and paddleboats can be rented from the park administrators (for $15.00 per hour in 2003). Anglers catch rainbow trout, kokanee, and whitefish.

Wildlife Viewing

Ornithologists are drawn to the hawks, owls, and swallows that live in the vicinity. In May you can hear tree frogs, while the summer nights bring a chorus of crickets. In the early fall, kokanee spawn in the lower waters of the creek. Rattlesnakes and gopher snakes that live in the area look similar, with the main difference being that rattlesnakes are poisonous. (I'd advise staying away from both of them!) There are illustrations on the information boards near the park change house suggesting that you should travel to Kelowna hospital if you are bitten. The small creek in the park is good for playing Pooh Sticks and for building small dams.

Family activities

This is a great place for children, with over 400 metres of sandy beach from which to enjoy the calm, safe waters. Sandcastles and moats are easily constructed here. As mentioned above, the numerous washed-up logs enhance the range of activities to be undertaken in and around the lake. Dozens of picnic tables are found in a large grassy area, and there is a change house, horseshoe pit, and adventure playground. The paved roads of the campground are cycling and rollerblading terrain. Small deposits of placer gold can be found in the creek, so remember to bring the gold-pan and a lot of patience. In 2003, a not-for-profit group from Kelowna offered interpretative programs over the summer, some specifically for children. A donation was suggested for the interpretive programs and a small fee payable for the kids club.

Rainy-day activities

It is difficult to imagine a rainy day in the Okanagan, but if you do have the misfortune to experience bad weather, the rapidly growing city of Kelowna (a name derived from the Okanagan First Nation's word for grizzly bear) has a number of commercial activities, including an excellent kids' park (including a water park), open from 9:00 a.m. to

9:00 p.m. during July and August, go-carts, paintball, an exotic-butterfly garden, orchards with guided tours, golf courses, and, of course, wineries. Even if the weather is really bad, the park's proximity to Kelowna means there is always something to do. There is an old paddlewheeler that sails past the campground and offers tours of the lake ($20.00 per adult, under age five free). It departs from Kelowna City Park, adjacent to the Ogopogo statue, which you (or your children) may wish to climb. Fintry Provincial Park, north of Bear Creek, is also well worth a visit and has lots of pleasant walks. Lake Okanagan Resort (a 10-minute drive north of Bear Creek) offers horseback riding, and jet ski rentals.

Summary

When travelling in this area, be sure to keep an eye out for the legendary Ogopogo, a lake serpent said to inhabit the waters. Aboriginal people call it *N'ha-a-itk* meaning "spiritually powerful in water." The best viewing spot is reported to be south of Bear Creek on the eastern side of the lake, 6 kilometres north of Okanagan Lake Provincial Park. It is believed B.C.'s answer to the Loch Ness Monster makes its home in an underwater cave in this region of the lake. If there is no accommodation upon your arrival at Bear Creek, consider camping in Fintry, one of B.C.'s newer parks. Bear Creek is my second-favourite camping spot in the Okanagan. It's larger than Ellison and therefore not so intimate, but it is so convenient to everything in Kelowna, yet still quiet. Its location makes it an extremely popular provincial park, so if you're planning a trip in July or August, make sure you have a reservation.

Okanagan Lake Provincial Park

I have to admit that Okanagan Lake is not my own personal preference (I prefer Ellison and Bear Creek), but data from BC Parks confirm it is the most popular provincial park in the Okanagan, with over 20,000 camping parties staying each year—so, what do I know? My biggest problem stems from the fact that it is located relatively near a busy road, so the noise of traffic is easily audible in some sections of the campground. Having said that, it does provide easy access to a central part of the Okanagan and has wonderful vegetation, superb facilities, excellent views, generally good weather, and a 1,000-metre beach that does not have the noise problem, so perhaps I am just too picky. This is a campground that does not give a get-away-from-it-all feeling, and in this respect it is similar to Haynes Point, just down the road (see next section), or Golden Ears in the Lower Mainland. It is a friendly family campground.

History

The park was established in 1955 and is unique in its development. In the 1950s more than 100,000 trees were planted on the barren, rocky hillside. Many of them were non-native ornamental trees such

This tranquil scene is in the northern campground at Okanagan Lake Park.

Keep a close eye on your little ones near these fire pits.

as Manitoba, silver, and Norway maples; Russian olive; Chinese elm; Lombardy poplar; and red, blue, and mountain ash. This eclectic collection, together with the natural stands of ponderosa pine and Douglas fir, provides a home to a rich variety of bird life (see "Wildlife viewing"). Each year the park's popularity grows, as does that of the whole Shuswap–Okanagan region.

Location

Okanagan Lake is in the Okanagan Basin, 24 kilometres north of Penticton, between the wonderfully named communities of Peachland and Summerland. The campground is on 81 hectares of hillside between the highway and the lake.

Facilities

Okanagan Lake has two campgrounds, both equipped with showers and pit and flushing toilets. There are 168 vehicle/tent spaces, 88 of them in the southern part of the campground, where the boat launch is located. Spaces in the southern campground range in desirability. Some have good views of the lake but are quite close together; others have the benefit of privacy provided by vegetation but are farther away from the lake. Those in the northern campground tend to be larger and more private. Situated on a hillside, higher sites are close to the road and experience traffic noise (but compensate by having excellent views), while others lower down the slope are quieter. The park is wheelchair accessible (and the disabled washroom is great for family showering). Reservations are taken and strongly advised. Both campgrounds maintain a lush green environment because of an excellent sprinkler system, but be careful where you leave precious items (or kids) as they could suddenly get soaked, as ours did at 8:00 a.m. while we were having breakfast at the picnic table.

Recreational activities

Hiking

A few small trails wind through the park between the campgrounds. A pleasant one-hour stroll can be taken along a lakefront on a sandy trail strewn with pine cones. Sections of the sandstone cliffs along this track have unfortunately been scarred by graffiti, but despite this eyesore, the route is flat, pretty, and quiet. When you take this walk you can decide the best bit of beach on which to spend the rest of the day. This trail is also good for cycling.

Fishing

There is good fishing for carp, burbot, kokanee, Rocky Mountain whitefish, and large rainbow trout. When we stayed there, we spent hours catching toe-biters with fishing nets bought from a dollar store in Kelowna.

Boating

A boat launch is situated at the southern campground, and all types of powerboats are permitted on the waters. This can mean that a quiet paddle with a toddler is ruined by the jet ski crowd.

Wildlife viewing

The diverse collection of trees attracts a variety of bird life, including hummingbirds, cedar waxwings, quail, red-shafted flickers, western meadowlarks, and Lewis woodpeckers. Gopher snakes and rattlesnakes are also found in the area.

The boys ride the bear at the Kelowna water park.

Kids and adults beat the heat at the water park.

Sam and Jack sit on Ogopogo's head, but he doesn't seem to mind.

Fishing in the warm waters of Okanagan Lake is heavenly.

Kekuli Provincial Park has a great playground.

Campers relax at the beach at the northern campground in Okanagan Lake Provincial Park.

Ever hopeful, the boys try their luck at fishing again.

A welcoming moose stands guard near the entrance to the Clearwater campground in Wells Gray.

Alberta's Dinosaur Provincial Park is in rugged country known as the badlands.

The boys enjoy the playground in Dinosaur Provincial Park.

Open wide and say "ah": Dad helps Sam inspect this dinosaur's mouth at the Drumheller Museum.

These log cabins are in Dinosaur Provincial Park.

A lone pooch sits on the pier at Cameron Lake in Waterton Lakes Provincial Park.

The guys play "Pooh Sticks" at Red Rock Canyon in Waterton Lakes Provincial Park.

The view from the bridge at Red Rock Canyon in Waterton is breathtaking.

Kids can easily manage the short hike to Blackiston Falls in Waterton.

The visitor centre at Peter Lougheed Provincial Park sits among snow-capped peaks.

RVs are a blessing when you're camping with young children. Like mom, the boys obviously enjoy climbing the ladder on the RV as well.

This playground in Okanagan Lake Provincial Park is typically much busier in the summer months.

Family activities

With over 1,000 metres of lakeside beach (the better sections are found nearer the northern campground) and access to what are supposed to be the warmest waters in the country, it is not surprising this location is so popular for swimming, windsurfing, sailing, sunbathing, and picnicking. The beach is somewhat stony, so water shoes are advisable. I tried to swim at the north beach and had great difficulty getting in, as the stones under my feet were so slippery. Watch out as well for a steep drop-off. Additional recreational options include a volleyball net and swings at the south campground.

Rainy-day activities

With such close proximity to centres of population, there is a wealth of things to do if it rains. Old McDonald's Farm is approximately 10 kilometres north on Highway 97, just after the other McDonald's, which, incidentally, has a play area. The Kettle Valley Railway in Summerland operates a quaint steam train over the summer months (this portion of the railway was not affected by the forest fires of 2003). It travels for about 10 kilometres through picturesque countryside. Each year this attraction seems to expand and employs some wonderful volunteers and enthusiasts who offer tons of information for the tourists ($15.00

per adult in 2003). There is a wine shop and vineyard just north of the campground just in case you are lucky enough to find a babysitter (or have brought the in-laws along). Just south of the campground at Okanagan Falls is a brilliant ice cream store with many flavours to choose from and where even the child-sized cones are huge. They also sell homemade fudge and other goodies—well worth the trip.

Summary

Okanagan Lake is an ideal camping spot for campers with children who are looking for a safe lakeside beach, or for those who want to have a central base from which to explore the Okanagan. It is the most popular campground in the region, offering all amenities in a pleasant environment. It is also very busy and in this respect is not to everyone's preference. During the summer months the temperatures in this region soar into the high-30s Celsius range, remaining there for weeks. The climate is extremely hot and dry, so if you are considering travelling to this region, my advice would be to avoid the busiest and hottest months (July and August) if at all possible and choose to vacation in May or September, when the weather is still good and the temperatures more bearable. These are, for me, the best times to visit this popular area of B.C., especially as the trees are in blossom from mid-April until the end of May, and most of the fruit (apricots, cherries, peaches, plums, pears, apples, and grapes) is still available in September.

Haynes Point Provincial Park

It is a great shame this campground in the heart of the Okanagan Basin is not larger, as it is an extremely popular location during the summer months; however, the climate ensures a pleasant stay for those who choose to visit in the spring and fall. I have to confess this is not my first choice because of its almost urban setting. That said, it is ideal for those who like the luxury of camping on a beach near a major centre of population, and if you have older children, it is ideal. The town of Osoyoos is within walking distance (although the 2-kilometre walk is not a good one). This advantage, together with the proximity of some of the Okanagan's finest vineyards and fruit farms, means that from June to November there are fresh fruit and vegetable stands at the sides of the highways, ensuring succulent produce is readily available for the camper's table. The season starts in May when the roadside stands sell fresh asparagus, which can also be found growing wild in the park.

History

This small 13-hectare park was created in 1962 and is named after Judge John Carmichael Haynes, who came to Osoyoos (originally known as Sooyoos) in the 19th century and became a renowned legal authority and landowner. He brought law and order to the goldfields of Wild Horse Creek, near Cranbrook, before moving in 1860 to assist the Okanagan area's gold commissioner and customs collector during the Rock Creek gold rush. He was subsequently appointed to the Legislative Council of B.C. and became a county court judge. Haynes built a large house in Osoyoos and established a ranch to serve the demands of the Cariboo gold miners. He lived there until his death in 1888. Historically, Aboriginal people lived, hunted, and fished in the area; two archaeological sites in the park tell their story. North of the park is a sandspit over which Highway 3 runs. This route forms part of the famous Hudson's Bay fur trading trail and has been used for centuries by fur traders, explorers, and miners. Today, orchards and vineyards dominate the area, with tourism contributing a major part of the economy. Veterans who settled in Oliver after the First World War established the first orchards.

Location

This very popular campground on Osoyoos Lake is found at the southern end of the Okanagan River Valley, in the rain shadow of the

Cascade Mountains, just 2 kilometres from the United States border and 2 kilometres from Osoyoos on Highway 97. The park encompasses a narrow sandspit formed by wave action that, together with a nearby marsh, juts out three-quarters of the way into Osoyoos Lake. Haynes Point is signposted from Osoyoos, although the signage near the park is not great, so be careful you don't miss the turn. All services are available in Osoyoos.

Facilities

It is little wonder this is a popular retreat, as all the 41 gravel camping spots are located on the sandspit, with over half having direct access to the beach only a few metres away. While there is not extensive vegetation, the spots are widely spaced. There are both flush and pit toilets, but no sani-station or showers. The park is accessible by wheelchair. Reservations are accepted and advisable as this is a popular location with both locals and tourists. One person I met here informed me that the locals have names for all the different campsites, adding a homey feel to the campground.

Haynes Point is a unique spit jutting out into Osoyoos Lake.

The view is idyllic from this picturesque camping spot.

Recreational activities

Hiking

A small trail leads through the marsh area of the park. Each time we visit, this trail seems to be under construction and is consequently getting longer and longer! It has great access to the wildlife-rich area. When the water is clear, you get excellent views from the trail of the lake's fish. This is a great kids' trail, as they can explore by themselves and not get lost.

Fishing

The lake is reputed to be the warmest in the country, making it a haven for up to 20 different types of fish. Rainbow trout, whitefish, and largemouth bass are abundant. Some of these huge specimens can easily be seen from a wooden bridge that runs over the marsh area.

Boating

Access to the warm waters of Okanagan Lake is one of the primary reasons people decide to come here; for boating enthusiasts the lake is perfect. The campground has a boat launch, and all types of powerboats and recreational craft are permitted on the lake, which regularly gets busy with windsurfers, paddlers, and powerboat operators. Expect noise from the jet-ski set as well.

Wildlife viewing

Those interested in wildlife may be rewarded by seeing the calliope hummingbird, Canada's smallest bird, as well as orioles, eastern kingbirds, and Californian quail. In the marsh area of the park, visitors may see canyon wrens and white-throated swifts. Other unusual creatures found in the area include spadefoot toads, painted turtles, rattlesnakes, and burrowing owls. Information boards at the park entrance give details about the appearance and habits of these animals.

Family activities

While adults enjoy this facility during the shoulder seasons, at other times it is primarily geared to those who have young children. Easy access to the safe waters of the lake, coupled with the excellent climate of the region, means many happy families need look no farther than the sun, sea, and gravelly sand provided at Haynes Point. For those who just visit for the day, a change house is available in the day-use area. The paved circular road is good cycling/rollerblading terrain, and of course, it is only a short bike ride to the town. The lake can also easily be accessed from the town of Osoyoos, where the beach is sandier and where ice creams are abundantly available.

An early-morning breakfast is the best way to fuel up for another fun-packed day.

Rainy-day activities

As mentioned above, only 2 kilometres away is the town of Osoyoos. A Spanish theme predominates here, with many stucco buildings and red-tiled roofs. A small museum is one of the town's few tourist attractions. Originally an 1891 log schoolhouse, it has a mixture of displays on topics including the history of irrigation, the history of B.C.'s provincial police force (long since replaced by the RCMP), bird specimens, and Aboriginal artifacts. Osoyoos is the fruit capital of Canada. The season starts in June with cherries, followed by apricots, peaches, plums, apples, and grapes. The area also has Canada's only banana farm and must contain the highest number of fruit stands anywhere in the country. The warm climate and lack of rain promote desert plants such as ponderosa pine, bear cacti, sagebrush, and greasewood. Just south of Oliver is a federal ecological reserve—a "pocket desert." It may be difficult to find, as when we visited there were no signposts, but once we discovered it, we found the area fascinating. It supports subtropical flora and fauna such as cacti, horned lizards, rattlesnakes, and burrowing owls. Wear good shoes to explore the area.

Summary

If you want to be sure of sun, sea, sand, and people during your summer vacation, make sure you book Haynes Point well in advance, as this campground is frequently full. It is a place for families, for boaters, or for people who just want to sit by a lakeside and watch others for the day. Haynes Point is not a place to visit if you want seclusion or quiet. One of the biggest disadvantages is that traffic noise or music from the nearby town can be easily heard. If you plan to stay in the summer months, be warned that the temperatures can be very hot for weeks, so pack the sunscreen. I think this campground is most suitable for parents with school-aged children, as it's small enough to let them run off and explore by themselves and gain independence without getting lost. The other real advantage here is the campground's proximity to the town, which has a number of fast-food options, so you don't always have to figure out what to barbecue for supper.

You're never too young to help with the camping chores.

NORTHERN B.C. AND THE ROCKIES

This section covers a somewhat eclectic collection of campgrounds I deem to be good family locations in less populated regions. I have selected two campgrounds in the Rockies: Kootenay National Park and Kikomun Creek Provincial Park; one in the Kootenays, Kokanee Creek Provincial Park; and one in Northern B.C., Lakelse Provincial Park. Camping in these campgrounds is a bit of a gamble, as you are more likely to experience bad weather and the camping season is typically shorter, but there is the advantage of fewer people, and for me these campgrounds offer a more realistic camping experience (which may or may not be a good thing, depending on your perspective of camping with kids). Other family camping recommendations may include: Moyie Lake, Premier Lake, Wasa Lake, or Yoho National in the Rockies region; Kentucky–Alleyne, Mount Robson, or Wells Gray in the central Interior of B.C.; and Paarens Beach, Tyhee Lake, Liard River Hotsprings, or Crooked River in northern B.C. In venturing to these places be sure to pack Gore-Tex™, fleece, and DEET, and go for an adventure!

Lakelse Lake Provincial Park

For those who crave mountain views and cool, clear lakes with sandy beaches at a campground offering all facilities, with the bonus of easy access to a mineral hot springs, this is the place to be. We booked into this campground when I was pregnant in mid-September 1998, planning to stay just one night before heading to my destination in the Queen Charlotte Islands. We ended up staying four nights because the road between Terrace and Prince Rupert was blocked by a landslide. What a perfect place to be delayed. In 2002, we returned with the children. Lakelse is a provincial park suitable for every age and every interest, with loads of activities within its boundaries and in the nearby towns. The biggest draw for me and my family, however, is Mount Layton Hot Springs, 3 kilometres from the park itself.

History

There are nine hot, odourless pools in the region. The Haisla and Tsimshian people who travelled the area centuries ago first discovered these pools. In 1904–05, a wagon road was built beside the springs to supply material for the construction of a railway that was to run from Kitimat to northern B.C. During the initial railroad exploration, which never came to fruition, a man named Bruce Johnson acquired the land and in 1910 built a hotel at the hot springs. Despite the lack of rail transportation, Johnson developed a successful business around the hot springs by advertising extensively in the United States. He ultimately built a second hotel and bathhouse at the lakeside, but hard times during the Great Depression, coupled with a fire, led to the abandonment of the venture. The springs remained undeveloped until 1958, when the facilities were renovated. They subsequently changed ownership a number of times, and in the early 1980s were completely renovated again and opened under the name Mount Layton Resort. Today this is one of the most developed hot springs in the province.

Location

In the midst of the majestic old-growth forest of the Skeena River watershed, ringed by mountains in the Kitimat Range of the Coast Mountains, and surrounded by a comprehensive range of facilities including the hot springs, this is an attractive campground for all ages. The park, 24 kilometres south of Terrace on Highway 37, is a beautiful

Surely this is every three-year-old's dream: a playground on the beach.

haven for the traveller. Services can be found either in Terrace or in Kitimat, 33 kilometres further south.

Facilities

The 156 large, well-organized, and well-maintained gravel campsites cater to every type of recreational vehicle and are set within a forest of cedar, hemlock, and Sitka spruce. There are full facilities here, including a sani-station, flush toilets, and showers. There are facilities for the disabled, and reservations are accepted. This is one of the best cared for campgrounds that we have stayed in.

Recreational activities

Hot springs

Mount Layton Hot Springs' odourless, colourless waters are reputed to be the hottest in Canada. During the summer the hot springs are open from 10:00 a.m. to 10:00 p.m. There is one large pool at 30 degrees Celsius (87 degrees Fahrenheit); a smaller, hotter pool at 41 degrees Celsius (106 degrees Fahrenheit); and a "turtle" pool for children at 32 degrees Celsius (90 degrees Fahrenheit). The turtle pool contains large, brightly coloured plastic animals that were originally used at Expo 86 in Vancouver. The park has five waterslides. A café, restaurant, and pub are all on site, and the admission price is reduced by a dollar if you are staying at the provincial park. This is a wonderful place to spend the day no matter what the weather is like. We visited with our children in May and were the only people in the pools.

Hiking

There are not many hiking possibilities adjacent to the park, although a 2-kilometre, self-guided nature trail called Twin Spruce Trail offers an easy walk through the forest.

Fishing

The fishing here is reputed to be fantastic. Both trout and Dolly Varden are frequently caught, and all five species of Pacific salmon, as well as steelhead and char, are available. In August, sockeye salmon spawn in William's Creek in the northern part of the park, and BC Parks literature boasts of "world class salmon and steelhead runs." There is excellent chinook and coho fishing in the nearby Skeena and Kitimat rivers; the towns of Kitimat and Terrace have numerous shops dedicated to every aspect of this sport. During our initial visit it appeared that 90 percent of the other campers were there to fish.

Boating

There is a large, paved boat launch in the park at Furlong Bay Campground. Powerboating, canoeing, waterskiing, and windsurfing are all popular activities.

Wildlife viewing

Mammals that inhabit the region include moose, wolves, coyotes, cougars, and black bears. The famous Kermode bear—a white-coloured black bear—is also native to the region, but is rarely seen except as an emblem on municipal property in Terrace. Over 100 species of birds have been identified here. In the Tsimshian language, *lakelse* means "freshwater mussel," so expect to find some of these while exploring the waters of the lake.

Family activities

Children will adore the soft sands of the beaches in this park, and in summer the lake's water warms up to temperatures that encourage swimming. Near the beach are a change house, playground, and numerous picnic tables. Paved roads wind throughout the campsite, which is a real draw for the older children who cycle or rollerblade on them.

Rainy-day activities

The town of Kitimat to the south offers tours of the world's largest aluminum smelter and also boasts B.C.'s oldest Sitka spruce tree, located an easy, child-friendly walk from the car park into the forest (watch out for the big bad wolf). The town's information centre is open throughout the year. To the north, Terrace is famous for "fishing and bears," and seems to be developing as a tourist town. There is a kids' indoor play space, should the weather turn really bad. During my first visit to Terrace I found a shop with a sign that read "prepared moose meat." I had never tasted moose and, thinking it could be interesting on the barbecue, I went in to buy some, only to be told by the proprietor that I had to go and kill the animal first; then he would prepare the meat ... I did not attempt it.

Summary

Lakelse is a delight to visit, providing a range of activities both within its boundaries and in the surrounding area. Families with young children will find it particularly enjoyable, as will anglers. It is easy to spend an entire day at the hot springs, and children (and some adults) will be entertained for hours on the waterslides and play areas available. The older generation should also appreciate the restorative waters of the springs, which are open well into the evening hours. During our first visit we spent a wonderful Wednesday evening in mid-September as one of four people enjoying the hot springs. My husband and I had races down the waterslides for an hour; then the only other couple in the place, who were both over 60, confessed they were jealous of our screams and enjoyment and followed our noisy example once we vacated the slides. Four years later we returned with a three-year-old and an 18-month-old and had just as much fun. As it was May and quite cool, we opted to stay at the hot springs resort, eat burgers and fries in the café, and then retire—exhausted but very clean and wrinkly—to our lodging to watch videos in the small bedroom. Sometimes even the most ardent campers have to decide that there are advantages to *not* camping.

Kikomun Creek Provincial Park

This is an excellent place for family camping if ever there was one. This campground feels to me like an English country estate with its large, open grasslands. A number of quiet, paved roads take you to locations in different regions of the park: the day-use area at Surveyors' Lake, the main Surveyors' Campground, the group camping area, South Pond Campground, the boat launch, and Koocanusa Reservoir. These different attractions and facilities are not closely packed together but are kilometres apart. The park consequently feels huge—much larger than its 682 hectares—just because you see so much of it as you go from place to place. This gives it quite a different feel compared to other provincial parks.

History

The park was established in 1972 to provide facilities for recreationists as well as to preserve an example of ponderosa pine/grassland habitat. The productive grasslands in and around the park were used initially by the Ktunaxa people, who hunted deer, moose, mountain sheep, goats, geese, and grouse, and then by the European settlers who set up cattle ranches. The Ktunaxa people named the creek 'Qikmin, a name that referred to its tendency to dry up or shrink in the summer months. The construction of the Libby Dam in Montana created the huge reservoir.

Location

Kikomun Creek is situated in the southern region of the Rocky Mountain Trench, 68 kilometres from Cranbrook. Turn off Highway 3/93 at Elko, 32 kilometres west of Fernie, and take the paved road 11 kilometres south. Some services are available at Jaffray, 11 kilometres from the park, but the nearest are at a private marina 4 kilometres from the park's entrance. The marina supplies gas, propane, fast foods, and has a grocery store.

Facilities

The quality of the 104 camping spots offered in the three campgrounds varies tremendously. In my opinion, by far the best location is Surveyors' Campground, a large campground with every amenity—including reservable sites, wheelchair accessibility, and showers—and spaces that can accommodate either the largest RV or smallest tent (tent pads available). Because of the sparse vegetation, many of these spaces feel

Kikomun Creek feels like an English country estate.

quite open, but they are far enough apart to be completely private. This campground is on two levels, close to two sandy beaches. The second campground is South Pond, which provides a regimented line of spaces with no privacy, although a large grassy area nearby invites you to pitch your tent. Only the basic amenities are offered here (pit toilets, firepits, picnic tables, water). This campground is close to the reservoir. The third location is basically the parking lot near the boat launch, aptly named Boat Launch Campground, on Koocanusa Lake. Again, only the basic facilities exist in this site, offering little aesthetically. Choose this campground if boating is your primary passion but be advised it is not at all kid-friendly. There is a sani-station at the main entrance to the park.

Recreational activities

Hiking

There are a number of easy hikes you can take here. Surveyors' Lake Trail is an easy 45-minute walk around the lake. Watch for painted turtles. Hidden Lake is a shorter 30-minute interpretative stroll, while the Great Northern Rail Trail is a route for both mountain bikers and walkers (one to three hours depending on your mode of transportation, age, and level of fitness). Hikers of every age group can complete all trails. The first two feature interpretative boards along the route, while the latter is the subject of a leaflet you can collect from the campground host (if there is one) or at the start of the trail in Surveyors' Campground.

Cycling

The park is a delight to cycle in, as there are not only quiet paved roads between the various campgrounds and day-use areas, but also a number of old roads and disused railway beds nearby. As mentioned above, the Great Northern Rail Trail is open to mountain bikers.

Fishing

The six lakes here—Surveyors', Hidden, Engineers, Skunk, Fisher, Muskrat, and Koocanusa—all have fishing opportunities. Koocanusa Lake is noted for kokanee, Rocky Mountain whitefish, cutthroat trout, and Dolly Varden, while smallmouth bass, eastern brook trout, and rainbow trout are more prevalent in the smaller lakes. During the fall, kokanee spawn in Kikomun Creek.

Boating

A concrete boat launch is provided at Koocanusa Lake. Powerboats are prohibited on the smaller lakes.

Wildlife viewing

The park is home to one of B.C.'s largest populations of western painted turtles, so-called because of the bright pattern they exhibit underneath their shell. A wander around Surveyors' Lake when the sun is out affords numerous opportunities to view these creatures soaking up the rays, while on a dull day their small faces can be seen bobbing in the water. Spotting these creatures can keep little ones entertained for hours. Interpretative boards around the lake provide interesting facts about these cute reptiles. Badgers, elk, black and grizzly bears, coyotes, cougars, and deer all inhabit the region. Birds seen in the park include osprey, mallards, red-tailed hawks, bald eagles, owls, and American kestrels.

A boat-launch campground overlooks Koocanusa Reservoir.

Family activities

This is an ideal place to sojourn if you have children. There are two gorgeous sandy beaches by Surveyors' Lake, and the waters of the lake are clear, clean, and quite warm. Young ones can spend hours building sandcastles, playing in the sunshine, or swimming to the offshore raft. There is an adventure playground near campsite 37 in Surveyors' Campground. We stayed in early June, and the waters were easily warm enough to swim in for both adults and children. If you end up doing nothing else, you'll love the beaches.

Rainy-day activities

Those who want to explore the local communities have many interesting options. The town of Fernie, a 40-minute drive from the park, has an interesting historical downtown core with buildings dating back to the 1890s. While in Fernie, take the historical walking tour, then visit the restored railway station for refreshments. Mount Fernie Provincial Park, 2 kilometres west of the town, is a good location for a picnic and walk. To the north of Kikomun is Fort Steele, which is well worth a visit whether you have children or not. This late-19th century settlement was almost a ghost town until the 1960s, when the government recognized its potential as a heritage site. Today almost 60 structures have been restored, including the North West Mounted Police camp (where children will be entertained climbing up to the fort's lookout tower), a huge water wheel, printing office, hotel, and bakery complete with delicious home-baked treats. It's a fascinating place, made even more interesting by the presence of guides in period costumes and the fact it's still a work in progress, with some buildings under renovation or about to be renovated. A must-see. Finally, the Kootenay Trout Hatchery on the Bull River, a 30-minute drive from the park, is a fascinating place to learn about the trout-rearing process. Forty percent of the trout needed to stock B.C. lakes are reared here.

Summary

We stayed here without children one hot weekday in early June when at 6:00 p.m. it was still warm enough to swim in the lake—which we had to ourselves, watched by a noisy osprey who had built a nest in a tree overlooking the waters. Four years later we returned with kids in tow, and I was sure it wouldn't live up to my memories. But it did, and it got better as I appreciated the many things to do near the park. Don't miss Fort Steele. You can easily spend a day there, and it's a fantastic space for kids of any age to run around and explore. We haven't visited Kikomun Creek in July or August, but I would anticipate it would be a wonderful place to make friends and have a thoroughly enjoyable camping vacation.

Kokanee Creek Provincial Park

It is rare to find a negative comment about Kokanee Creek Provincial Park. Some campgrounds are in fantastic locations but away from major centres of activity, so campers must bring their own entertainment; others have little to offer in their own environment, but are conveniently situated for exploration of the surrounding area. Kokanee Creek provides hundreds of activities both within its boundaries and in its immediate area. And its huge, white, sandy beach makes it one of the best lakeside campgrounds in the province. It is easy to spend two weeks here and not run out of things to do, even if it rains.

Kokanee Creek is the centre of the kokanee salmon spawning activity, which takes place in late August and September. When we first stayed one September it was not just the bright red salmon that were putting on a show. Their performance in the water was surpassed by a couple of ospreys who circled overhead, then dove into the waters of the creek only a few feet away from our vantage point, precariously flying away with huge salmon in their beaks. The spectacle was straight out of a *National Geographic* television program, although it is sad that a few of these fish, who have travelled so far just to spawn, will meet their demise so close to their destination, The area is noted for having one of the highest osprey populations in North America.

History

Kokanee means "red fish" in the Ktunaxa language and is the name given to the freshwater salmon that spawn in large numbers in the area. First Nations people inhabited the area many years ago and harvested these fish for the winter. At the beginning of the 20th century the region became popular with newcomers as gold and silver deposits were found in the surrounding hills and creeks. Legends tell of prospectors with names such as "Dirty Face Johnson" and "Dutch Charlie" who explored the area in search of precious metals. This exploration led to the development of some sizeable towns, such as Nelson. Kokanee Creek Provincial Park was created in 1955.

Location

Kokanee Creek is in the Kootenay area of the province—an area often overlooked by tourists, who prefer to vacation in the Rockies or on the coast. This means the region is generally quieter than others, a real advantage if you choose to travel in the summer months. The provincial park is set in the beautiful scenery of the Slocan Range of the Selkirk Mountains, on the western arm of massive Kootenay Lake, 19 kilometres north of Nelson on Highway 3. Services are conveniently located in Nelson or Balfour (12 kilometres to the south).

Facilities

Kokanee Creek provides 132 wooded camping spots in two locations: Sandspit (numbers 1 to 113) and Redfish (114 to 132). Redfish is closer to the road, making Sandspit my personal preference. Sandspit may also be preferable for campers with kids as it is nearer the beach and playground, with a few sites overlooking the playground, and it does not entail crossing a main road to get to the beach. Kokanee Creek is home to the West Kootenay Visitor Centre, so the facilities here are good, including flush toilets, a sani-station, and disabled access. There are no showers. Reservations are accepted. The camping spots themselves are large enough to accommodate every type of recreational vehicle, and group camping is also available.

Recreational activities

Hiking

There are a number of small (20- to 60-minute) trails that zigzag around the park, taking explorers to views of the spawning channels and to the beach. For those who demand a more serious stretch of the legs, Kokanee Glacier Provincial Park is a 32,000-hectare area with an extensive trail system. A leaflet describing these hikes is available from the visitor centre.

Fishing

The fishing here is reputed to be second to none for both rainbow trout and kokanee, and the locals claim that the world's largest rainbow trout (4.5 kilograms, or10 pounds) was landed here. Dolly Varden, char, burbot, and whitefish are also regularly taken from the lake and nearby waterways. There are also, of course, ample opportunities for your children to use their nets and try for toe-biters in the many small streams.

Boating

The campground is equipped with a boat launch, and the lake is popular with kayakers, jet skiers, canoeists, powerboaters, water skiers, and windsurfers. Fortunately its huge area means it never gets crowded, although the noise of the jet skiers can be irritating if you are planning a quiet time on the beach.

Family activities

This provincial park is a delight for anyone with children, who will not want to return home from this paradise. There are a number of beautiful, long, sandy beaches and a safe swimming area, changing rooms, picnic facilities, and children's play area. The visitor centre has displays on salmon spawning, and when we visited one June it had a live-bear trap on display outside. The numerous paved roads in the campground are great for cycling and rollerblading.

Rainy-day activities

One of the joys of staying here is the number of activities to do and sights to see close at hand—pursuits suitable for every taste and every age group. The community of Nelson is one of the oldest and certainly one of the prettiest in B.C., with the highest concentration of heritage buildings in the province. In Nelson you can visit the museum, take a self-guided walking tour, or use the excellent indoor swimming pool.

Kaslo, 50 kilometres to the north, is a small community with a nine-hole golf course, coffee shops and cafés, and the SS *Moyie*, the last sternwheeler on Kootenay Lake, which is now a museum. For those interested in ghost towns and early prospecting history, Sandon, further west along Highway 31A, is a delight to visit. It is slowly being renovated by a number of dedicated volunteers. When we visited, a gangly 14-year-old youth enthusiastically showed us the hydroelectric power room, complete with huge generators brought across from Manchester, England. There was also a tea shop for refreshments and a souvenir store. The museum is highly recommended, and the town site is a great place for kids of any age to explore.

Ainsworth Hot Springs, 29 kilometres north of the park, boasts warm, therapeutic mineral pools and a system of caves stretching into the rock face to explore. Our kids found the cave experience "too spooky" but loved the hot pools. The hot springs were completely renovated in 1998 and make a great place to visit even if the weather is bad. Cody Caves Provincial Park (no camping facilities) is located in the Selkirk Mountains above Ainsworth Hot Springs, just 11 kilometres along a good forest road off Highway 31. Visitors to the park can view spectacular cave formations including stalagmites, stalactites, waterfalls, draperies, rimstone dams, and soda straws. You are provided with the necessary protective clothing and hard hats when you take the highly

This big, bad bear trap is NOT to be used for locking away noisy children!

informative tours offered by BC Parks. Not recommended for kids under seven years old.

What used to be the longest free ferry ride in the world, across Kootenay Lake from Balfour to Kootenay Bay, is just a 20-minute drive north from the campground. If you have the opportunity, take a morning ferry and have breakfast—the trip is entertaining and the price is unbeatable.

Summary

If you are searching for a campground where you can pitch a tent for a week or more, and which offers swimming, sunbathing, and water sports in addition to numerous other activities within an hour's drive, then look no farther than Kokanee Creek. It is an idyllic family lakeside location. One of the times I enjoy most is dusk, when the day trippers are gone and there are quiet trails to walk on while I watch the sun go down and the stars come out. For those of us who live in the Lower Mainland, the nine-hour drive to the Kootenays may be off-putting, but it is well worth it. In addition to the camping, I regard the town of Nelson as the most beautiful in the province. We stayed at Kokanee Creek with our two young children late one September, when most of the sites had been closed, picnic tables were stacked ready for storage, and there was no one to collect our fee. We had to wear fleece to explore the campground comfortably and take walks, but the place was all ours; so it remains very special to us.

Kootenay National Park

Another campground that offers mountain scenery and a nearby hot springs can be found in the Rockies. Kootenay National Park appeals to both adults and children. While the adults may be most struck by the spectacular scenery and wildlife, the kids will love the hot springs and the various small walks that can be easily completed. During my first visit to Kootenay National Park I met a parks representative who told me that Kootenay was often overlooked in comparison to its well-known neighbours, Banff and Jasper, with just over 1.2 million visitors a year compared to Banff's 4.7 million and Jasper's 2.2 million. For anyone who has experienced the crowds at Lake Louise or Banff in August, this can only be good news. Kootenay's 1,406 square kilometres are rich in variety. It is the only park to contain both glacial peaks and cacti within its boundary; but these are not the only rewards. Radium Hot Springs, numerous gorges, waterfalls, mountains, and two major river systems (the Vermilion and the Kootenay) add to its glory, as do a host of interesting excursions for the tourist. In 1985 UNESCO designated Banff, Jasper, Yoho, and Kootenay National Parks as World Heritage Sites, officially recognizing the beauty and significance of the Rocky Mountains and creating one of the largest protected mountainous areas in the world.

History

Interpretative boards at Marble Canyon detail the area's 500-million-year-old geological development. Human habitation is a little more contemporary, but it still goes back a long way. Aboriginal people have travelled, hunted, and camped in the region for over 11,000 years. They recognized the magic of the hot springs and regarded them as sacred waters, a place to cure illness and gain spiritual peace. The first registered owner of the hot springs was

A footbridge crosses over Marble Canyon.

Roland Stuart, an Englishman who purchased 160 acres of land, including the hot springs, for $160 in the first decade of the 1900s. The government of Canada expropriated the land and springs from Stuart in 1923 and has been responsible for them ever since. Kootenay National Park opened in 1920 and owes its birth to Highway 93, the first road to cross the central Canadian Rockies, which in turn led to the development of motorized tourism. The province of B.C. gave the park to the government of Canada in return for the road.

Location

The park encompasses land of the Continental Divide and the Columbia Valley. The west entrance is 1 kilometre north

This scenic road cuts through the rocks in Kootenay National Park.

of Radium, and the park stretches along 90 kilometres of Highway 93 as it heads north. All services can be found at Radium, and there is also a restaurant, store, and information office at Vermilion Crossing, operated by Kootenay Park Lodge and located roughly in the centre of the park.

Facilities

Three campgrounds operate within the park's boundaries. The largest and most popular is Redstreak, which is open from early May until the end of September and has 242 sites, including 50 with full hookup and 38 with electricity. Flush toilets, showers, and a sani-station are available here, as are facilities for the disabled. Redstreak is my personal preference as not only does it have all amenities, but also it is possible to walk to the hot springs from here (about 15 minutes). This campground is not signposted very well; you enter it by exiting the park and taking a paved road beside the RCMP station in Radium on Highway 93/95. Stay here if you want easy access to the hot waters.

McLeod Meadows Campground is open from mid-May until mid-September and is 26 kilometres north of Radium between Meadow Creek and Kootenay River. It has 98 spaces, flush toilets, a sani-station, but no showers. The spaces are large enough for every size of RV and are in a lightly forested area, with some of the best locations being close to the river. The third campground is Marble Canyon, open from mid-June until early September, 86 kilometres north of Radium. With 61 spaces set in a dense, subalpine forest, it is the quaintest of the campgrounds, although it has flush toilets and a sani-station but no showers.

Recreational activities

Hot springs

Radium Hot Springs is probably the best known of B.C.'s hot springs and among the most developed. It is are also the most radioactive hot springs in Canada, but don't worry—this radioactivity is too weak to be harmful. The pools are immensely popular; over 400,000 people use the facilities each year. There are two developed open-air pools: a hot soaking pool with temperatures up to 47.7 degrees Celsius, and a cooler swimming pool, 24 metres long, with hot water cooled by creek water to 27 degrees Celsius. The smaller, hotter pool nestles into the walls of the cliff, and it is possible

The pools at Radium Hot Springs are immensely popular.

to look up to see bighorn sheep on the ledges above the pool. You can access the pools via a trail from Redstreak Campground or by vehicle. The hot springs are very popular, especially during the summer months. When we visited in July, we found that opening time at 9:00 a.m. was a good time to go to avoid the crowds. For those who arrive unprepared, locker rooms, showers, and swimsuit and towel rentals are all available. This is a great place for kids and fully accessible for the disabled.

Hiking

One of the joys of Kootenay Park is the number of short, easy, yet fascinating trails that can be undertaken by any age group. Among the most popular are the following: Olive Lake, a boardwalk trail with interpretative signboards and a fish-viewing platform, 13 kilometres from Radium; Paint Pots (85 kilometres north of Radium), a 1.5-kilometre trail leading to cold, iron-laced mineral springs that bubble up through the earth and stain it a deep ochre colour; and Marble Canyon, a kilometre-long interpretative trail, easily completed with young children, through an impressive narrow canyon of grey limestone that leads to a pounding waterfall. (Remember the camera if you do this one.) There are over 200 kilometres of trails in the park, so numerous day hikes are possible in addition to overnight excursions. One of the most popular day hikes is a 10-kilometre, five-hour-return trek to Stanley Glacier through a dramatic landscape of fire and ice. Details of all these routes can be obtained from the park information centre, 3 kilometres north of Radium, or at the Vermilion Crossing visitor centre, 63 kilometres north of Radium.

Fishing

While it is possible to fish for brook and rainbow trout, whitefish, and Dolly Varden, most of the streams and rivers are fed by glaciers, so the water is too cold to yield high fish populations.

Boating

Only non-motorized craft are permitted on the lakes and rivers in the park.

Wildlife viewing

In addition to 179 species of birds found in the park, Kootenay is home to 5 to 10 grizzly bears, 15 to 25 black bears, 5 to 10 wolves, 50 to 75 elk, 50 to 70 moose, 100 to 140 bighorn sheep, and 250 to 300 mountain goats. I did not count them; these figures come from a publication put out by the park. The best time to see these creatures is in the early morning and at dusk.

A quiet moment of reflection is enhanced by Kootenay National Park's ban on motorized boats.

Family activities

With no developed beach or natural waterfront, Kootenay is not a prime family location. However, Redstreak Campground does provide easy access to the hot springs and pool, has an adventure playground, and is near to the town of Radium, so if you have children to entertain, there is plenty to do. The numerous short trails scattered throughout the park are easy for children to complete and are immensely educational. Lake Windermere, a 15-minute drive south of Kootenay National Park, has two lovely beaches and relatively warm waters, and is easily accessible from James Chabot Provincial Park (no camping), so if your children want water-based activities, head here.

Rainy-day activities

The communities of Radium and Invermere offer a number of commercial activities including golf. Radium has a number of restaurants and fast-food outlets. Invermere is a pretty town whose main street is lined with flowers in the summer. If you have not had enough of hot pools, head further south to check out Fairmont Hot Springs, which has a restaurant and lots of grass for the kids to play on and has seen considerable development over the last few years.

Summary

For me there are two sides to Kootenay National Park. The southern portion near Radium is busy and somewhat commercialized. During the summer months it is crowded as tourists congregate around the therapeutic waters of the hot springs. The other side of Kootenay is its vast expanse away from the hot waters, which provides a cornucopia of things to see and do. It is easy to spend two to three days travelling slowly through the park, exploring its natural wonders, walking the trails, and camping at the different locations.

For those who want access to the hot springs but wish to retire to a quiet, small campground in the evenings, Dry Gulch Provincial Park is an interesting option. Five kilometres south of Radium on Highway 93/95, this little-known haven has 26 tranquil sites that to my eye are superior to those at Redstreak. There are no showers or hookups, and access to the hot springs requires a drive, but it is a more private campground.

Waterton Lakes National Park townsite (Heritage House collection).

ALBERTA

I have not camped extensively in Alberta, but each year I manage to become acquainted with a few more campgrounds and become impressed with services which seem to be standard in this province but which are not so readily available or have been cut in B.C. (e.g. small stores in the campgrounds, interpretive programs, laundromats, and showers that are coin operated but hot). Now that I am a parent, I really appreciate these services. My selections include two provincial parks, Dinosaur and Peter Lougheed, and one national, Waterton. Other recommendations could have included the national park giants of Banff and Jasper in the Rockies or Writing-on-Stone Provincial Park and Little Bow Provincial Park, both in the southern part of the province.

Dinosaur Provincial Park

All kids love dinosaurs, so what better place to take them than Dinosaur Provincial Park, a UNESCO World Heritage Site in the Red Deer Badlands area of Alberta, which is an excellent family location packed with dinosaur fun. The landscape here is unique: a rugged country of erosion with the Red Deer River running through it, featuring amazing rock sculptures known as hoodoos. This landscape is home to scorpions, black widow spiders, and rattlesnakes, so explore in good footwear. But it is not all barren; cottonwood trees offer shade in the campground (and allergies to those who suffer), and there are large grassy areas to play on and to pitch the tent. We stayed in late June when there were very few visitors, but it was still very hot and the mosquitoes were out. DEET and sunscreen must be the order of the day for July and August. Although the parks staff did say that some years they are mosquito-free, my 16 bites had me doubting this boast.

History

Dinosaur Provincial Park contains one of the richest dinosaur fossil reserves in the world. Over 500 complete dinosaur skeletons have been found in the park. Seventy-five million years ago the area was a lush tropical region of swamps and rivers—ideal dinosaur habitat. When the dinosaurs died their bodies became encased in layers of mud and silt that built up and eventually turned to sedimentary rock, burying the creatures. The Ice Age stripped away and eroded this rock, revealing the dinosaur bones. Erosion has continued, and so now dinosaur bones are sticking up everywhere (almost). The area has been awarded World Heritage Site status for three reasons: because of the dinosaurs, because it contains an extensive tract of badland landscape, and because it is home to a large number of cottonwood trees growing on the banks of the Red Deer River, which also accommodates a large variety of plants and animals.

The Red River runs through Dinosaur Provincial Park.

Location

The park is only 73 square kilometres in area, and is 48 kilometres northeast of the town of Brooks, about a two-hour drive on Highway 1 from Calgary. The sizeable town of Brooks has all services (including a McDonald's with a play space). Dinosaur Provincial Park is signposted from Brooks and is accessed on paved roads.

Facilities

This campground has everything! One hundred and twenty-six sites, including some that have power access. In 2003, campers paid $15.00 for standard sites, $18.00 for those with power. Spaces are quite open and large, with picnic tables, firepits, and water. Gravel roads ribbon through the campground, which means everything can get a bit dusty. There are pay showers ($1.00), a laundry, and firewood is for sale at the lovely on-site store. Reservations are accepted (for a $6.00 reservation fee) and are strongly recommended (403-378-3700). When we stayed, there was a campground host. If Dinosaur is full, try Kinbrook Island Provincial Park, 15 kilometres south of Brooks, which is situated on the warm waters of Lake Newell and is an alternative where you can swim. Dinosaur Provincial Park has a service centre where you can purchase

The songbirds around the campsite at Dinosaur Provincial Park like to sing at the first hint of daylight.

supplies, ice cream, ice, wood, and even a cooked breakfast or lunch. It's not too commercial and is a great facility for a camper who is not used to finding such a service at a campground. Be warned: it can get very crowded when a busload of local Grade 3 students coincides with the Discover Alberta over-60s bus tour!

Recreational activities

Hiking

The lovely thing about this park is that the trails are easy, varied, and not that long; you can do them all in a day and still have time left for other activities. Two trails are wheelchair accessible: the Cottonwood Trail (one hour), which meanders along the Red Deer River and is good for bird watching, and the Prairie Trail (15 minutes), near the park's entrance. My favourite is the Badlands Trail (45 minutes) as it's so varied and has great views of the hoodoos. There's also the Fossil Hunters Trail (40 minutes) where the kids can hunt for bones, and the Coulee Viewpoint Trail (45 minutes), which has good views. Remember to wear good footwear and take plenty of water.

Cycling

Bikes are prohibited on the trails, but the many roads that ring around the campground make for good kids' cycling.

Wildlife viewing

During our brief stay we saw rabbits and mule deer. The bird life here is extensive; apparently the cottonwood trees and the underbrush of dogwood, rose, and Saskatoon berry support one of the largest populations of songbirds in Alberta (nuthatches, yellow warblers, and so on). They all like to sing at the first hint of daylight, which can be at 4:30 a.m. in June—believe me.

Family activities

In addition to the five guided walking trails described above, there are a couple of playgrounds to keep the kids entertained. The Royal Tyrrell Museum Paleontology Field Station is also in the park. Here, for a small fee, you can see into their lab where the dinosaur bones are prepared, as well as view large dinosaur bones on display. There is also a theatre that shows a dinosaur film nightly (free admission at 7:00 p.m. each

Jack and Sam take five next to a dinosaur skeleton.

There's lots to see at the Royal Tyrell Museum Paleontology Field Station.

evening). The centre offers its own kids' activity book for no charge, and it's ideal for kids over age seven. One of the most popular events is the two-hour bus tour into the badlands, led by a parks interpreter ($6.50 for adults, $4.25 youth 7–17, under 6 are free). The bus stops on several occasions and you get out to see dinosaur bones everywhere. I found this to be really amazing while my three-year-old got a little bored. But we were on and off the bus so much that this varied activity kept him distracted. Remember sunscreen and water. The field station also offers guided hikes, each over two hours long and designed for older children; one is a fossil safari and the other goes to a *Centrosaurus* bone bed. All tours and guided hikes can be reserved.

Rainy-day activities

A visit to Dinosaur Provincial Park is not complete without another visit—to the dinosaur capital, Drumheller. A two-hour drive away, Drumheller is home to the Royal Tyrrell Museum with dozens of complete dinosaur skeletons, dinosaur bones, interactive displays, and theatres. The town of Drumheller also has the world's largest dinosaur: a 45-metre-long, 26-metre-high *Tyrannosaurus rex*. Visitors climb 106 steps up for a view out of his gaping jaw ($2.00 fee). Now, what kid could resist that? The T. Rex is outside the visitor centre, but there are almost 30 dinosaurs positioned throughout the town. A *Styracosaurus* is positioned in front of the drugstore and an *Apatosaurus* guards the entrance to the IGA supermarket, and there is also a wicked looking *Triceratops* near the town's theatre. While some adults may find it all a bit tacky, kids love it.

Summary

To do justice to this provincial park you need at least a couple of days. Parks literature states that any place 75 million years in the making deserves your time. If you do plan a visit, reserve ahead, as the campground and bus tours fill up quickly. We all really enjoyed our stay in early June. The birdsong in the morning, seeing deer and rabbits on the evening stroll, the smell of the lavender bushes en route to the Badlands Trail, the fantastic array of cactus flowers, and the unique scenery, all made it a trip we will not forget. However, I have no idea whether I would be quite as enthusiastic if I had visited in July, when all the camping spaces were taken and the temperature was at 40 degrees Celsius with no breeze and the mosquitoes in their best biting mood. Residents of Alberta may be used to the heat, but for a B.C. family making the trip, my advice is to go for June or September. In 2002, 85,000 people visited Dinosaur Provincial Park, 70 percent more than in 1992, so obviously many don't mind the heat. The only other drawback we found was the lack of water-based activities, although we did all did have fun running through the campground's irrigation system. The sprinklers are turned on in the late afternoon, ensuring that the grass stays green, kids get wet, and the mosquitoes keep happy.

Waterton Lakes National Park

I did not visit Waterton when the weather was brilliant, but as we arrived and took our first steps to the visitor centre, a red fox casually meandered up the adjacent path toward the women's washrooms, just as two women emerged. They were as surprised by the four-footed visitor as we were. From this initial encounter I knew Waterton was special, and it is. My children expected "Little Bear" and his animal friends to be around the next corner! I do not care for the populated national parks of Jasper and Banff much, for although the scenery is spectacular, the crowds are not. By contrast, Waterton is not as large, is somewhat out of the way, and so is much quieter but just as spectacular. The town of Waterton is *much* less crowded than Banff, Jasper, or Lake Louise and is consequently a far more pleasant environment to spend time. This is a national park for every age group, and with the majestic Prince of Wales Hotel dominating the skyline, one where I definitely plan to return to one day without kids.

History

Waterton became Canada's fourth national park in 1895, 10 years after the first was established at Banff. It meets Montana's Glacier National Park at the border of United States and Canada, and in 1932 both were designated the world's first International Peace Park, acknowledging the bonds of peace and friendship between the two countries. In 1995 they were given World Heritage Site designation because of the fantastic glacier-carved landscapes, the over 1,200 species of plants and animals living within the boundaries, and the rich

We pause to pose and admire the view in Waterton Lakes National Park.

biological diversity. The elegant Prince of Wales Hotel, reputed to be one of the most photographed hotels in Canada, was built in 1926 by the Great Northern Railway's president, Louis Hill, and it retains much of its 1920s charm (which is, of course, lost on any under-five you take there).

Location

Waterton Lakes National Park is located in the southwest corner of Alberta, 264 kilometres from Calgary, and 130 kilometres from Lethbridge. If travelling from the Lower Mainland of B.C., schedule two full days to get there. It is a relatively small 500-square-kilometre park, but in that space there is more plant and animal life than in Banff and Jasper combined (960 species of plants, 250 species of birds, and over 60 mammals).

Facilities

There are primarily three campgrounds at Waterton. The main Waterton Township Campground is open May to October, is the only one with showers, and is located in the town. It is *very* open and can get somewhat windy. While it accommodates all sizes of RV and tents (238 spaces), the openness offers little privacy, but if you want to be near the cappuccino bars or restaurants, it is the place to be. We stayed at Crandell Mountain, which was fantastic, with large sites and excellent views; it offered no showers but had well-kept bathrooms with flush toilets and sinks. There are 129 spaces here, and it's ideal for kids of any age as there is so much to explore just in the surrounding undergrowth or by cycling on the gravel roads. Similarly, Belly River Campground offers the same type of camping experience but is much smaller (24 spaces). Fees for the campsites range from

This is our superb camping spot at Crandell Mountain.

$16.00 to $22.00 and there is a $6.00 charge for firewood. In 2003, the sites couldn't be reserved, but this policy is under review.

Recreational activities

Hiking

The park boasts over 200 kilometres of trails, and what we really appreciated was the number of trails that were easily accessible, not lengthy but nevertheless interesting. From the visitor centre, try the 1.2-kilometre climb up Bears Hump Trail—well worth it for the views of the lakes (but not advised for very young children). The Linnet Lake Loop Path is wheelchair accessible, so it's ideal if your offspring are in a stroller. This trail offers lots of interpretive information along the way. Our kids really enjoyed the Red Rock Canyon Trail (easily completed by the three-year-old) and the 1-kilometre return walk to Blackiston Falls through a forest with evidence of bear scat, and across bridges ideal for playing Pooh Sticks. When you get to Blackiston Falls, you will find wonderful photo opportunities. There are also a number of far more strenuous hikes. Free trail information is given at the visitor centre.

Boating

For the young and the young at heart, canoes, kayaks, paddleboats, and rowboats can be rented at Cameron Lake from a very funky little outlet that also sells candy bars, coffee, and fishing supplies. Boating, waterskiing, and scuba diving are popular on Upper and Middle Waterton lakes, but be warned—the water is cold. Interpretive boat cruises, which have been in operation since 1927 and which take about two and a half hours, seem popular with visitors to Waterton, but can work out to be quite costly for a family.

Cycling

Bikes are available for rent in the town of Waterton (including those large "family" bikes where two parents pedal a huge monstrosity without gears and the kids ride in style). The town itself is flat and easy to explore.

Family activities

Waterton has a fantastic golf course should your children be old enough to enjoy this sport, or, if they're at the other end of the scale, a playground ideally situated opposite an ice cream store. Parks staff offer interpretive programs in the summer at the two main campgrounds, and during the peak summer months a number of kids' programs are offered; check out

Scenic Blackiston Falls in Waterton Lakes Provincial Park are easy to get to.

the visitor centre when you arrive to find what's available. For the family that fishes, cutthroat trout, rainbow trout, arctic grayling, northern pike, and whitefish can all be caught. The town itself is a nice place to wander and window shop, and there is a nice stroll on the Lakeshore Trail from Waterton itself.

Rainy-day activities

Unfortunately, you may really need this information, since Waterton is reputed to have Alberta's highest average annual precipitation (1,072 millimetres) with April, May, and June being the wettest months. As mentioned above, the Prince of Wales Hotel is well worth a visit and serves (I am told—we didn't test it) a wonderful "high tea" from June to September. There's a small movie theatre in town and a heritage museum. Although we stayed when it was rainy, we found one of the most enjoyable things to do with young kids was to take slow drives and stop at all the markers, get out, get wet exploring, and then move on. Canada's first oil well is situated in the park, as are a number of other spots of interest along Red Rock Canyon Road and Akamina Parkway. If you really need to escape the elements, drive for 90 minutes toward Lethbridge, and north of Fort Macleod on Highway 2 you will find the Head-Smashed-in Buffalo Jump historic site. Here is a wonderful museum of First Nations' heritage that children and adults alike will find extremely stimulating and informative. The building itself is a really interesting design, built into the rock. When you arrive at the entrance, three huge buffalo stare down on you. There is also an excellent theatre and a few small trails—a very kid-friendly place.

Summary

The disadvantage to Waterton Lakes National Park is that there is no beach or warm waters, and if you stay for more than three days you'll probably need to wear Gore-Tex™ at some time. The advantages,

The name says it all: Head-Smashed-in Buffalo Jump historic site.

though, are the spectacular scenery, brilliant wildlife, and gorgeous wildflowers that seem to dominate every hillside not covered with forest, a number of easy walks, and a lovely camping experience. Waterton is renowned as the place "where the mountains meet the prairies." The four main lakes—Lower, Middle, and Upper Waterton, and Cameron— can easily be accessed by car, and the roads provide ample opportunities for picnicking and exploring. Waterton Lakes National Park is a wonderful place to introduce your kids to a spectacular environment, and even if they do go home remembering only who found the largest slug, or whose Pooh stick was the best flowing in the fast rivers, or, as in our case, where the plastic Batman toy was lost, you'll feel like your parental batteries have been recharged by camping in this remarkable park.

Peter Lougheed Provincial Park

One of the real joys of this provincial park, the largest in Alberta, is the choice of six vehicle-accessible campgrounds within its boundaries, all of which offer quite distinctive camping experiences amongst the wonderful Kananaskis Country. This is a park for those who love cycling and hiking, but it's also great for families as it offers a number of interpretive programs, has a gorgeous visitor centre and on-site services, and sits amongst snow-capped peaks, glacial streams, picture-postcard lakes, and wonderful forests, all within an hour's drive from Calgary.

History

Aboriginal people used the Kananaskis Valley for thousands of years as a hunting ground for bison, elk, and deer. The name Kananaskis derives from a legend of an Aboriginal man who received a very heavy blow to his head from an axe, but then recovered. Upon hearing this legend, John Palliser, an early explorer who visited the region in 1857, named the river Kananaskis; now Kananaskis is often translated as "meeting of the waters." In 1978 Alberta premier Peter Lougheed officially dedicated Kananaskis Country and Kananaskis Provincial Park. In 1986 the park

Peter Lougheed Provincial Park is located in beautiful Kananaskis country.

Cycling and hiking among the snow-capped peaks are favourite activities at Peter Lougheed.

was renamed Peter Lougheed Provincial Park in honour of the premier whose vision of a protected wilderness recreational area for Albertans led to its creation.

Location

The 508-square-kilometre park is located in the centre of Kananaskis Country, 46 kilometres south of Highway 1 on Highway 40, about an hour's drive from Calgary. It is part of the Canadian Central Rockies. Peter Lougheed is one of a number of provincial parks that exists within Kananaskis Country; however, some others don't offer camping facilities.

Facilities

Peter Lougheed has six vehicle campgrounds (as well as six backcountry campgrounds and two group campgrounds); almost 600 camping spaces exist for every size of vehicle. The most popular campgrounds (and the ones with showers) are Boulton (118 spaces) and Elkwood (130 spaces). These are also the campgrounds that offer interpretive programs in the evenings. When we visited we preferred to stay in the less crowded Lower Lake campground (104 spaces and playground), which had easy access to the lake. Canyon Campground is further away from the interpretive programs and the lake, but has easy access to a scenic reservoir (50 spaces), and when we stayed in late June on a weekday this was the quietest campground, with only two spaces taken. Mount Sarrail (44 spaces) and Interlakes (48 spaces) are ideal if you want easy access to the lake and fishing opportunities. There is a small store and restaurant at Boulton. Campsites at Boulton can be reserved by calling 403-591-7226, or emailing www.kananaskiscamping.com. All campsites are large and, with the exception of some at Canyon, are in a forested environment. Firewood can be purchased from the campground administration.

Recreational activities

Biking

This really is the place to be if you love cycling, with over 100 kilometres of bike trails and over 12 kilometres of paved bike trails (much appreciated by those with toddlers in tow). This paved track is ideal if your kids are riding behind in a trailer, but be warned—much of the paved track is not on the level. The best place to start your journey on the paved track is from the visitor centre. This trail then ribbons its way by Upper Kananaskis Lake and includes sections of the Lodgepole, Wheeler, and Lakeside Trails. If you need more of a challenge, try the 24-kilometre Smith-Dorrien Loop Trail. The visitor centre can provide maps and advice.

Hiking

As with all large provincial parks there are trails to suit every need and ability. The visitor centre sells a leaflet for $1.25 that has all the routes and maps. There are a number of interpretive trails ideal for kids. Try Kananaskis Canyon, a 1-kilometre-long loop, or for a really good view of a cirque and a geology lesson, go for Black Prince Cirque, a 4.5-kilometre loop.

Fishing/Boating

Although we didn't catch anything (or see anyone else catch anything) our dollar-store fishing tackle was put to good use in the lakes next to the campground during our after-dinner strolls. Brook, cutthroat, rainbow, and bull trout as well as mountain whitefish can all be caught. Boat launches are available at the day-use areas of Upper Lake and Canyon.

Family activities

The visitor centre, with fantastic interactive displays and huge stuffed animals, is a delightful place for kids to explore. It also gives advice on where to position your child in order to get the best photo. In addition to the displays, there is a lounge with huge picture windows overlooking a grassy meadow. As mentioned above, the park offers a number of interpretive programs on Friday, Saturday, and Sunday nights during the summer months. These often take the form of plays and skits, providing education through entertainment to every age group. There are two playgrounds in the campgrounds at Lower Lake and Boulton.

Rainy-day activities

When we were there, it rained, so we headed off to explore Kananaskis Village. I had anticipated it to be a smaller version of Whistler or Jasper. Not at all. The only saving grace was the brand new "Tot Lot," a playground for kids, which was so unused we had to make three deer go away from the slide before our kids could use it, and the climbing equipment still had its bar codes on it, giving us the impression the Tot Lot had not seen a lot of tot use. There was a small café, a post office, but little to see or do. There is, of course, the famous golf course, reported to be one of the best in the world, should you decide to remortgage your house and play golf. To the north of the park, Boundary Ranch offers horseback riding excursions.

Summary

Although we stayed when the weather was not great, my kids really loved the adventure that Peter Lougheed Provincial Park offered. Here, they could safely wander from the campsite into the muddy low-lying areas to discover secret trails. After toasting marshmallows one night, we went to the lake to look for moose and to fish; then the next night, we stayed up and went to the amphitheatre for a discussion on bears, complete with sound effects that had everyone in the audience enthralled. For the camper, Peter Lougheed Provincial Park offers six different venues to try, which translates to six different environments for your children to explore. It is this vast size and variety of sites, as well as the fact it is so close to Calgary, that makes camping here so popular with Albertans.

Jayne Seagrave's
Camping British Columbia
A Complete Guide to Provincial and National Park Campgrounds

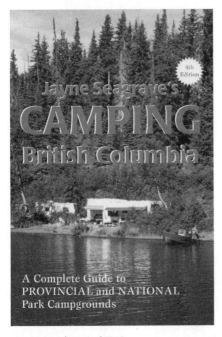

In this revised, updated edition of her best-selling guide, Jayne Seagrave once again brings her unique perspective and extensive outdoor experience to help define the ever-changing scene.

Seagrave's in-depth, first-hand accounts of her visits to parks in all regions of the province include interesting historical, environmental, and recreational facts that are sure to enhance campers' experiences, as well as countless practical tips on selecting a campground, what to take, how to stay safe, and how to take advantage of the reservation system. This edition also includes suggested tours, new photographs, and informative website addresses.

Camping/Travel B.C.
6 x 9   240 pp
1-894384-54-7
$19.95   sc

"... a much needed addition to the guide books available on BC ... informative and entertaining."
—*Powell River Town Crier*

"... goes beyond detailed information ... pragmatic advice on reservations, what to take, potential hazards, cookery tips and facts."
—*Island Tides*

"I wish I'd had this book for the last 20 years. I'll keep it for the next 20. It's a gem on camping info."
—Ron MacIsaac, Shaw Cable's *What's Happening?*

Handy little activity books to take with you when you go camping with kids.

Critters for Kids
1-895811-69-4
8.5 x 11   80 pp each
$8.95 - $9.95   sc

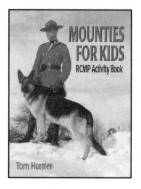

Mounties for Kids
RCMP Activity Book
8.5 x 11   48 pp
1-894384-10-5
$7.95   sc

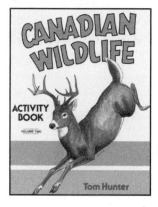

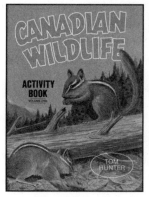

Canadian Wildlife
Activity Books
Vol. 1   1-894384-17-2
Vol. 2   1-894384-18-0
Vol. 3   1-895811-66-X

www.heritagehouse.ca

Handy little story books to take with you when you go camping with kids.

Jim Challenger's Family Library

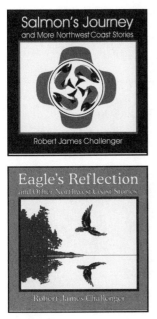

In *Salmon's Journey*, Jim Challenger's fourth collection of stories based on Canadian nature themes, the author/illustrator provides 20 new stories, expressing a philosophy of respect for the environment. Victoria's *Times Colonist* praised Challenger's earlier work, saying he "knows how to write for the oral storyteller; the written words slip easily off the tongue."

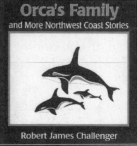

Eagle's Reflection	1-895811-07-4
Orca's Family	1-895811-39-2
Raven's Call	1-895811-91-0
Salmon's Journey	1-894384-34-2

8 x 8   48 pages

$9.95   sc

Jayne Seagrave lives in Vancouver with her husband, Andrew, and sons Jack and Sam. She holds a Ph.D. in criminology and, in conjunction with her husband, owns and manages the Vancouver Tool Corporation. She moved to British Columbia from England in 1991.